A Concise
Introduction to
Symphony

ALSO AVAILABLE

(by Noel Kantaris)

A Concise Introduction to Symphony

by
Noel Kantaris
and
Phil Oliver

BERNARD BABANI (publishing) LTD.
THE GRAMPIANS
SHEPHERDS BUSH ROAD
LONDON W6 7NF
ENGLAND

PLEASE NOTE

© 1990 BERNARD BABANI (publishing) LTD

First Published – February 1990

British Library Cataloguing in Publication Data:
Kantaris, Noel
   A concise introduction to Symphony.
   Microcomputer systems. Software packages. Symphony
   I. Title II. Oliver, P.
   005.36'9

ISBN 0 85934 215 8

Typeset direct from disc by Commercial Colour Press, London E7.
Printed and Bound in Great Britain by Cox & Wyman Ltd, Reading

ABOUT THIS BOOK

This Concise Introduction to Symphony was written to help the beginner. The material in the book is presented on the "what you need to know first, appears first" basis, although the underlying structure of the book is such that you don't have to start at the beginning and go right through to the end. The more experienced user can start from any section, as the sections have been designed to be self contained.

Symphony is an integrated package containing five major types of applications; spreadsheets, graphics, database management, word processing and communications. The package is operated by selecting commands from menus or by writing special 'macros' which utilise the Lotus Command Language to chain together menu commands. Each method of accessing the package is discussed separately, but the emphasis is mostly in the area of menu-driven command selection.

The book was written with the busy person in mind. You don't need to read hundreds of pages to find out all there is to know about the subject, when a few pages can get you working quite adequately! Therefore, it is hoped that with the help of this small book, you will be able to get the most out of your computer, when using Symphony, in terms of efficiency and productivity, and that you will be able to do it in the shortest, most effective and informative way.

ABOUT THE AUTHORS

Noel Kantaris graduated in Electrical Engineering at Bristol University and after spending three years in the Electronics Industry in London, took up a Tutorship in Physics at the University of Queensland. Research interests in Ionospheric Physics, lead to the degrees of M.E. in Electronics and Ph.D. in Physics. On return to the UK, he took up a Post-Doctoral Research Fellowship in Radio Physics at the University of Leicester, and in 1973 a Senior Lectureship in Engineering at Camborne School of Mines, Cornwall, where since 1978 he has also assumed the responsibility of Head of Computing.

Phil Oliver graduated in Mining Engineering at Camborne School of Mines in 1967 and since then has specialised in most aspects of surface mining technology, with a particular emphasis on computer related techniques. He has worked in Guyana, Canada, several Middle Eastern countries, South Africa and the United Kingdom, on such diverse projects as: The planning and management of bauxite, iron, gold and coal mines; rock excavation contracting in the U.K.; international mining equipment sales and technical back up; international mine consulting for a major mining house in South Africa. In 1988 he took up a Senior Lectureship at Camborne School of Mines in Surface Mining and Management.

ACKNOWLEDGEMENTS

We would like to thank colleagues at the Camborne School of Mines for the helpful tips and suggestions which assisted us in the writing of this book.

TRADEMARKS

CONTENTS

INTRODUCTION

Symphony is a powerful versatile software package which is suitable for business, scientific and engineering users. It is an integrated program containing five major types of applications; spreadsheets, graphics, database management, word processing and communications. All these activities take place on a single spreadsheet, but are carried out by the use of a different window type for each environment. Multiple windows, representing multiple activities, can be viewed at the same time, the main limitation being the amount of working memory available in your computer.

Symphony's menu system, the 'user interface', is similar to that of Lotus 1-2-3, but because of the range of functions, and the power of the program, it can seem rather daunting to the new user. The basic rule is that menu functions common to all five environments are accessed by pressing a {**Services**} key (F9). Whereas the menu controlling the functions of each separate environment is accessed, from that environment, by a {**Menu**} key (F10). To change between the different environments a third menu system is activated by the {Type} key (Alt-F10).

It is assumed here that you have followed the instructions accompanying the software, relating to its installation on the hard disc of your computer, or its use from a floppy drive. If you are using an already installed package on hard disc, then it is most likely that the files which make up the complete package will be found in a sub-directory on your computer's hard disc, and that the program can be invoked by typing either **Access** or **Symphony** at the root directory's prompt. An appropriately written batch file would then locate the sub-directory in which the program's files reside and load the 'Symphony Access System' into memory. It is also hoped that you are using Symphony 2.0, as with earlier releases you may find that some sections of the book will not be strictly relevant to you.

If your system is correctly implemented, you should now be in the 'Symphony Access System' which is headed by the display shown below.

```
Start Symphony
Symphony  Tutorial  PrintGraph  Install  File-Translate  Exit
```

The bottom line displays the Access menu which lists all of the options available to you.

1

Note that the option "Symphony" is highlighted and that the highlighted bar can be moved by pressing the right arrow, left arrow or the spacebar. Also note that as the highlighted bar moves, the description line (first line in the boxed area) changes. The description line explains what will happen if that particular option is selected. Selection of an option can also be made by typing the first character of an option given in the menu.

Loading the Symphony Program:
To load Symphony, highlight the first option on the "Access" menu and press the <Enter> key. This will load the program into your computer's memory, after first displaying the Lotus licence agreement. When the program is loaded the default working environment is the spreadsheet, and the border below is displayed.

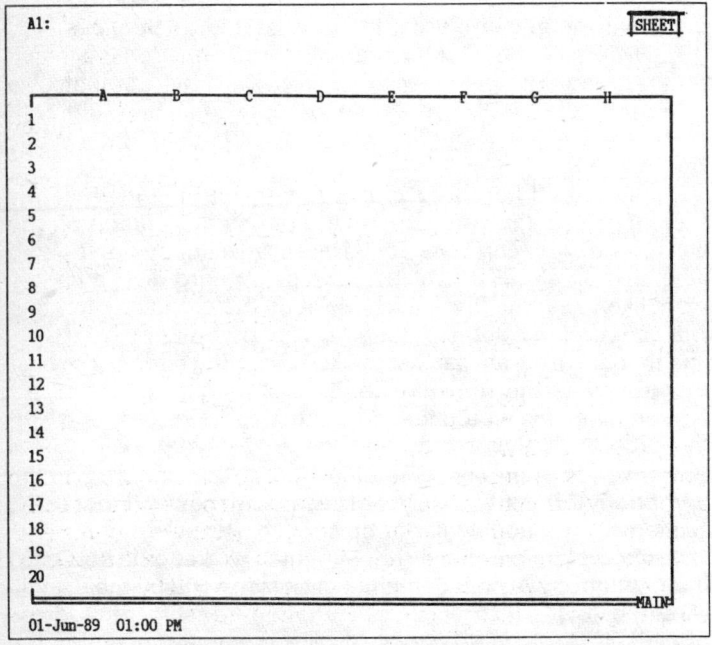

Symphony has just set up a huge electronic page, or spreadsheet, in your computer's memory, many times larger than the small part shown on the screen. Navigation around the spreadsheet is achieved by use of the four arrow cursor keys. Each time one of these keys is pressed, the highlighted bar

2

moves one position right, down, left or up, depending on which arrow key was pressed. The <PgDn> and <PgUp> keys can also be used to move vertically 20 rows at a time. A spreadsheet can be thought of as a two-dimensional table made up of rows and columns. The point where a row and column intersect is called a cell.

When you have finished navigating around the spreadsheet, press the <Home> key which will bring you to the Home cell, (A1), which is the top left-hand corner of the spreadsheet. This is known as the Home position. Individual cells are identified by column and row locations (in that order), with a maximum size extending to 256 columns and 8192 rows. The columns are labeled from A to Z, followed by AA to AZ, BA to BZ, and so on, to IV, while the rows are numbered from 1 to 8192. The reference points of a cell are known as the cell address. The location of the highlighted bar is constantly monitored by the 'cell indicator' which is to be found on the top left hand corner of the screen. As the highlighted bar moves, this indicator displays the address of the cell.

By now you will have noticed that there are several areas on your screen; the area within which you can move the highlighted bar is referred to as the working area of the spreadsheet. The letters and numbers in the highlighted border form the reference points. It is worth noting that the highlighted bar cannot be moved into these border areas of the spreadsheet. If you try, the speaker beeps. Finally, the very top and bottom lines of the screen are reserved for displaying certain 'control information'. For example, on the very top right-hand corner of the screen, the 'mode indicator' displays the word 'SHEET' in inverse video, and the date and time appear on the last line of the screen. For a list of indicators, see Appendix A.

The {Goto} Command:
Sometimes it is necessary to move to a specific address in the spreadsheet which is so far from the present position that using the arrow keys would take far too long to get there. To this end, Lotus has implemented the **F5** function key as a {Goto} command. For example, to jump to position HZ5000, press the {Goto} key (F5) which will cause Symphony to ask for the address of the cell to which it is to jump. This request appears on the second line on your screen, in a position immediately below the cell indicator. The default address is the address of the highlighted bar. Now, typing HZ5000 and pressing <Enter>, causes the highlighted bar to jump to that cell address. To return to the Home (A1) position, press the <Home> key.

3

To specify a cell address you must always key one or two letters followed by a number. The letters can range from A to IV corresponding to a column, while the numbers can range from 1 to 8192 corresponding to a row. An address outside this range will cause the word ERROR to flash in the 'mode indicator' (top right-hand corner of the screen), the speaker to bleep, and a message to appear on the screen telling you of the invalid range. To correct this situation you must first exit from it by pressing the <Esc> key. In fact, the <Esc> key can be used to cancel a command and escape from a situation before an error occurs.

Entering Information in a Worksheet:
We will now investigate how information can be entered into the spreadsheet. But first, return to the Home (A1) position by pressing the <Home> key, then type in the information given below. As you type, the characters appear in the control area of the spreadsheet under the cell indicator. Type the words:

```
PROJECT ANALYSIS
```

If you make a mistake, press the <BkSp> key to erase the previous letter or the <Esc> key to start again. When you have finished, press <Enter>. Note that what you have typed now appears in cell A1, even though part of the word ANALYSIS appears to be in cell B1. Typing any letter at the beginning of a cell results in a 'label' being formed which is automatically preceded with the apostrophe (') character. Pressing <Enter> inserts the information as a 'label' into the highlighted cell. If the length of a label is longer than the width of a cell, it will continue into the next contiguous cell.

Now move the highlighted bar to cell B3 and type

```
Jan
```

and press <Enter>. Use the right arrow key to move to the next cell (C3) and type

```
Feb
```

but this time press the right arrow key. The result of this action is to cause the information you were typing to be entered into the highlighted cell and at the same time move the highlighted bar to the next cell. Now move to cell A4 and type

```
\=
```

and press <Enter>. Note that typing the backslash (\) and then following it with any character, causes the whole cell width to be filled with that character.

Now move to cell B4 and type \- as above, then to cell C4 and repeat. The result should be a double line extending the full width of cells A4 to C4.

Finally, move to cell A5 and type

`Consult:`

then enter the numbers 14000 and 15000 in cells B5 and C5, respectively.

What you should have on your screen now is the following:

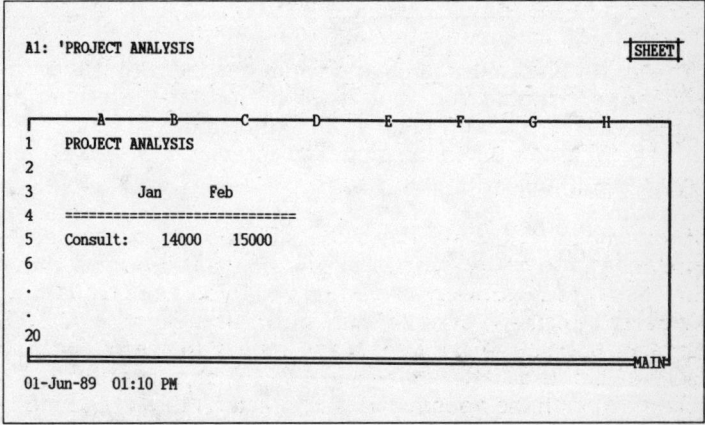

Note how the labels 'Jan' and 'Feb' do not appear above the numbers 14000 and 15000. This is because by default, labels are left justified, while numbers are right justified.

The {Edit} Command:
One way of correcting the looks of this spreadsheet is to right justify the labels 'Jan' and 'Feb' within their respective cells. To do this, move the highlighted bar to cell B3 and press the {Edit} key (F2), which will allow you to edit the contents of the cell. The cursor is now moved into the control area below the cell indicator displaying:

`B3:    'Jan`

with the cursor at the end of the label. Use the left arrow key to move the cursor under the apostrophe (') character and delete it with the <Del> key. Then type the double quote (") character which will be inserted to take the place of the deleted apostrophe. On pressing the <Enter> key, the label is now right justified within its cell.

Thus, in general, to edit information already in a cell, move the highlighted bar to the appropriate cell and press the {Edit} key (F2). The cursor keys, as well as the <Ins> and <Del> keys can be used to move the cursor and/or edit information as required. Other function keys have the following meaning:

Symbony from LOTUS ⌐ Alt + Esc	COMPOSE	⎵WHERE⎴	⎵⎵SPLIT⎴⎵	⎵CENTRE⎴		⎵LEARN⎴	⎵ZOOM⎴	⎵STEP⎴	⎵DRAW⎴		⎵SWITCH⎴	⎵TYPE⎴	
	HELP	EDIT	ABS	CAPTURE		GOTO	WINDOW	USER	CALC		SERVICES	MENU	
	F1	JUSTIFY F2	INDENT F3	ERASE F4		F5	F6	F7	F8		F9	F10	

These will be discussed as and when needed. But it is worth noting that should you need help, at any stage, pressing the {Help} key (F1) will bring up a context related help screen. The first help screen, when the mode indicator is on 'SHEET', offers help on the following items:

SHEET Commands:
Punctuation settings:
Formulae:
Strings:
Labels:
Numeric Display Formats:
@Functions:
Help Index:

The above are menu options and can be selected by moving the highlighted bar to the required choice and pressing the <Enter> key. There is an extensive list of sub-menus under each menu choice. As the {Help} command is context sensitive, pressing it while in the middle of entering another command will bring up the help screen relevant to that command.

Saving a Worksheet:
Now, let us assume that we would like to stop at this point, but would like to save the work entered so far, before leaving the program. First, let us return to the Home position by pressing the <Home> key. Then we need to use the {**Services**} provided by Lotus. {**Services**} are called up with the **F9** function key, while the options under {**Menu**} are called up with the **F10** key or the front slash key (/).

6

Thus pressing the {**Services**} key (F9), will produce a 'Lotus' style horizontal menu at the top of the screen, as follows:

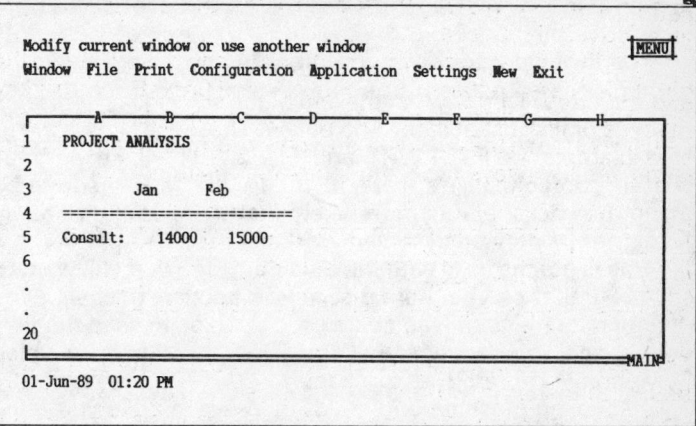

The main line of the menu lists the options available, while the line above describes the option that is currently highlighted. This menu operates the same as the menu we came across when we first loaded the 'Symphony Access System'. Thus, the highlighted bar can be moved by using the right or left arrow key, the <Home> key or the <Spacebar>. Note that the 'mode indicator' at the top right-hand corner of the screen now reads 'MENU'.

To make a menu selection, say **F** (for **F**ile), we can either move the highlighted bar over the fifth option and press <Enter>, or simply press the first letter of the desired option (**F** in this case). We shall use this last method to select 'File' as it is quicker. If you make a mistake, simply press the <Esc> key and try again. On selection of 'File', the mode option on the top right-hand corner of the screen changes to 'FILES' and we are presented with another menu of options within the 'File' option.

Pressing **S** (for **S**ave), causes the following to appear within the top control area:

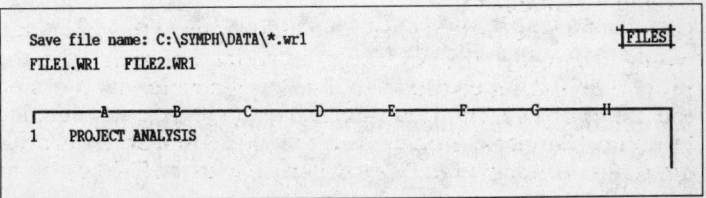

The second line now tells you the default sub-directory to which data files will be saved. This, in the case of a hard disc system, could be the

`C:\SYMPH\DATA`

sub-directory. The *.wr1 at the end of the second line indicates the type of files listed in the line below. These are shown in our last example as FILE1.WR1 and FILE2.WR1 which perhaps contain someone else's work. If you are the first person to be using the package, it is more likely that there will not be any filenames of previously saved work.

If this is not the case with the data path, and you still want to save your files on your hard disc, it is imperative to change the default data file path (see next section), so as to save the files you create into a separate directory from that in which Symphony program files are kept.

To save the present contents of memory to a file you must either highlight an existing filename with the help of the cursor keys or type a new filename. If you choose to save your work under an existing filename, you will be asked whether you would like the contents of the file on disc to be 'Replaced' by the contents of the current memory. If you do, type **Y** to confirm your decision. If, on the other hand, you choose to save your work under a new filename, then the moment you start typing its name, the menu of existing filenames disappears and what you type replaces the *.wr1 at the end of the data path. To end this session, type

`PROJECT1`

and press the <Enter> key. The extension .WR1 will be added automatically by the program.

Summarising:- To save worksheet files do the following:

First, make sure that the mode indicator is on 'SHEET'. If not, press the <Esc> key as many times as necessary to achieve it, then press

F9	to invoke the {**Services**} menu
F	to select **F**ile
S	to select **S**ave.

Symphony asks for a filename to save under. The first data file saved previously in the specified drive\path is highlighted. Pressing <Enter>, requires confirmation.

Changing the Default Data Drive/Path:
Assuming you want to change the default drive/path to which your data is to be saved, do the following:

First, make sure that the mode indicator is on 'SHEET'. If not, press the <Esc> key as many times as necessary to achieve it, then press

F9   to invoke the {**Services**} menu
C   to select **C**onfiguration
F   to select **F**ile.

The mode indicator now reads 'EDIT' and on the first line on the screen, the current directory for data is displayed. To change this, to say the A: drive, type <Esc> followed by A:.

If, on the other hand you wanted to save your work on the C: drive, then provided a \DATA sub-directory to the main Symphony directory already exists, then add \DATA to the displayed default directory shown on the screen which, in the case of a computer with a hard disc, may be C:\SYMPH, and press <Enter>.

If you want to make this change permanent, then press

U   to **U**pdate the configuration setting.

From now on data will be saved and retrieved from the newly 'Updated' drive:\path. Finally, press the <Esc> key to return to the 'SHEET' mode. Each time <Esc> is pressed, Symphony returns to the previous sub-menu. Repeating the process will eventually return you to the 'SHEET' mode.

Erasing a Worksheet:
To erase a worksheet from memory and also clear the screen, save your work first, and then press

F9   to invoke the {**Services**} menu
N   to select a **N**ew worksheet
Y   to confirm the command.

Your work will disappear irretrievably. Always use this command to clear memory and screen of unwanted information before starting with a new worksheet. Never switch off your computer in order to clear its memory of unwanted work! Computers are best left running for the entire working period, as switching them on and off too many times in a day can cause premature hardware failure.

Retrieving a Worksheet:
An already saved worksheet file can be retrieved by the following command sequence. Press

F9   to invoke the {**Services**} menu
F   to select a **F**ile operation
R   to select **R**etrieve.

Symphony asks for a filename to load. The first data file saved in the specified drive\path is highlighted. Pressing <Enter>, retrieves this highlighted file, or pressing the right arrow cursor key highlights the next file. When a file is retrieved it replaces anything that was already held there. Therefore, you don't have to erase the memory before retrieving a new worksheet.

Symphony provides a facility for merging files in various ways. To do this from the 'SHEET' mode press

F9   to invoke the {**Services**} menu
F   to select a **F**ile operation
C   to select a **C**ombine operation

which reveals a sub-menu with **C**opy, **A**dd and **S**ubtract options in it.

Exiting a Symphony Session:
To quit the program, press **F9** to display the {**Services**}. Make sure that this is done when the mode indicator is on 'SHEET'. If it is not, press the <Esc> key as many times as is necessary for the mode indicator to change to 'SHEET'. Then press **F9** to display the {**Services**} and press **E** (for **E**xit).

Before exiting the program, Symphony prompts you again, because if you exit a session without saving your worksheet you will lose any changes made. The prompt is of the form

End Symphony session? (Select "No" if your work isn't saved)
No Yes

with the highlighted bar over the 'No'. Pressing **Y** (for **Y**es) ends the Symphony session and the program returns either to the 'Symphony Access System', to the DOS operating system, or to whatever menu was used in the first place to load Symphony. If the program returns you to the 'Symphony Access System', type **E** to **E**xit.

FILLING IN A WORKSHEET

We will use, as an example of how a worksheet can be built up, the few entries on 'Project Analysis' which we used in the last chapter. If you haven't saved the PROJECT1 example, don't worry as you could just as easily start afresh. If you have saved PROJECT1, then enter Symphony and, at the 'SHEET' mode, press

F9   to reveal the {**Services**}
F   to select **F**ile
R   to select **R**etrieve.

or in abbreviated form, {**Services**} **F**ile **R**etrieve, which is the format that will mostly be used throughout the rest of this book. If there are a lot of files on disc, press **F10** to display them in more than one line on screen.

   Now highlight PROJECT1 and press <Enter> to display the worksheet on screen. Then use the **F2** function key to 'Edit' existing entries or simply retype the contents of cells (see over) so that you end up with the following worksheet.

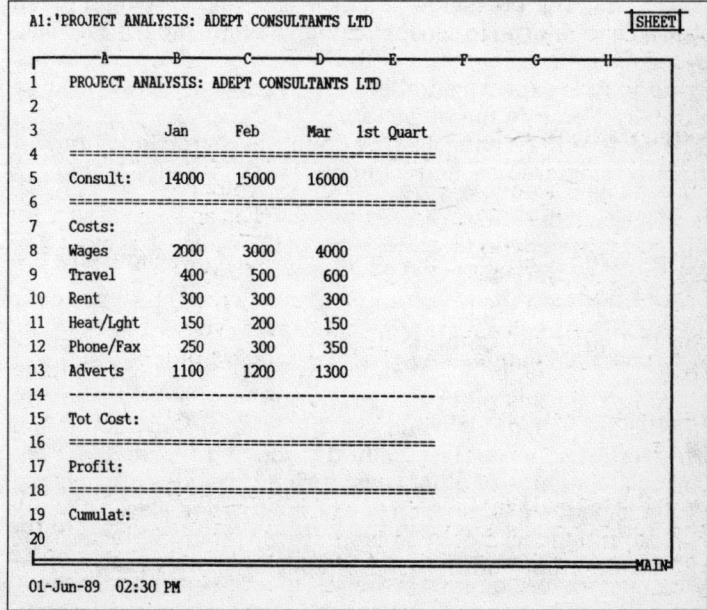

Formatting Labels:
Labels can be formatted with the help of the following prefixes:

'	to left justify
"	to right justify
^	to centre
\	to repeat a character.

With these in mind, the information in cell A1 (PROJECT ANALYSIS: ADEPT CONSULTANTS LTD) was entered left justified. In fact we just typed in the label in A1 without preceding it with the apostrophe. Similarly, all the labels appearing in column A were just typed in as shown. This is the default entry mode for labels, with Symphony automatically adding the apostrophe.

The labels relating to the months in cells B3, C3, D3 and E3 were entered with the caret (^) prefix, so as to. centre them within their respective cell. Note that had we attempted to just type

1st Quart

in cell E3, on pressing <Enter> Symphony would have beeped and refused to accept the information into the cell. This is because the label starts with the numeral 1 which causes Symphony to expect a number. However, what follows is not a number, therefore the objection.

Repeated information, like the double line stretching from A4 to E4 was entered by first highlighting cell A4 and typing

\=

On pressing <Enter> the equal character (=) sign fills the entire cell.

The {Menu} Copy Command:
To copy information to other cells we could repeat the above procedure (in this particular case entering the \= characters) within each cell, or we could use the {**Menu**} **C**opy command which is by far the quickest method of copying information from one cell to a range of other cells. ({**Menu**} options are invoked by pressing the **F10** function key or the forward slash {**/**} key). This command is not restricted to repeated character-type information, but can be used equally well with numbers or formulae.

To copy the contents of cell A4 to the range of cells from B4 through E4, ensure that you are in the 'SHEET' mode (press <Esc> until you are), then move the cell pointer to A4, and type {**Menu**} Copy.

At this point, you'll be asked for the range to copy **FROM**. In this case, the cell pointer (note that the mode indicator has changed to 'POINT') is at the cell we want to start copying from and the entire copy range is highlighted (i.e. the range is given by A4 to A4), therefore press

<Enter>   to confirm the range

which will cause Symphony to ask you to enter the range to copy **TO**. Now press

Right Arrow   to move to the starting location of the range
.   (period) or <Tab> to anchor the first target cell
Right Arrow   to select and highlight target cell range
<Enter>   to confirm target range.

If you make any mistakes and copy information into cells you did not mean to, then use the {**Menu**} Erase command.

The {Menu} Erase Command:
To erase a range of adjacent cells, highlight the first cell and invoke the {**Menu**} Erase command, then press the Right, Left, Up or Down arrow key a number of times to highlight the row or column range to erase, and press

<Enter>   to confirm selected range.

To erase a block of cells, highlight one corner cell of the block and press

.   (period) to anchor first corner of block
Arrows   to complete block of cells
<Enter>   to confirm block selection.

Entering Numbers and Formulae:
When numbers are entered into a cell, or a reference is made to the contents of a cell by preceding the cell address with an arithmetic operator, or a Symphony function, preceded by the @ sign, is entered into a cell, then the mode indicator changes from 'SHEET' to 'VALUE'.

Returning to our example of PROJECT ANALYSIS, move the highlighted bar to B5 and start entering the 'consultancy' income of the company. As soon as the first number is typed

13

into the line below the cell indicator (the number 1 of the 14000), the mode indicator changes to 'VALUE' and when the complete amount is typed in, pressing <Enter> inserts it into the specified cell, right justifying the number within the cell width. Now complete typing in the rest of the amounts into cells C5 and D5.

We can find the 1st quarter total income from consultancy, by highlighting cell E5 and typing

`+B5+C5+D5`

and on pressing <Enter> the total first quarter consultancy income is added from the above formula and the result placed into E5. Notice that the above formula is preceded by a plus (+) sign. Had we not typed this first '+' sign into the formula, Symphony would have mistaken the formula for a label and no calculation would have resulted.

Now complete the insertion into the worksheet of the various amounts under 'costs' and then save the result into the file

`PROJECT2`

Before going on any further, remember that saving your work on disc often is a good thing to get used to, as even the shortest power cut can cause the loss of hours of hard work!

Entering Functions:
In our example, writing a formula that adds the contents of three columns is not too difficult or lengthy a task. But imagine having to add 20 columns! For this reason Symphony has an in-built summation function (for others see Appendix B) in the form of

`@SUM( )`

which can be used to add any number of columns (or rows).

To illustrate how this function can be used, move the highlighted bar to E5 and type

`@SUM(`   which changes the mode indicator to 'VALUE'

then use the arrow keys to move the cell pointer (note that pressing an arrow key changes the mode indicator to 'POINT') to the start of the summation range (B5 in this case), then press

to anchor the starting point of the range

and use the arrow keys to move the cell pointer to the end of the summation range (in this case D5). What appears under the cell indicator is the entry

```
@SUM(B5..D5
```

which has to be completed by typing the closing bracket and pressing <Enter>. The first few lines on your screen should look as follows:

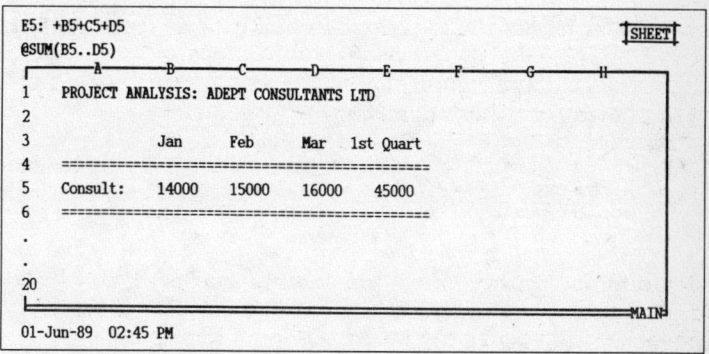

Now use the **C**opy command to replicate the function from cell E5 into the target range E8 through E13. To achieve this move the highlighted bar to E5 and invoke the {**Menu**} **C**opy command, then press

<Enter>	to confirm highlighted copy range
Down Arrow	to move to beginning of target range
.	to anchor the first target cell
Down Arrow	to select and highlight target range
<Enter>	to confirm target range.

Immediately this command is confirmed, its execution causes the actual sums of the 'relative' columns to appear on the target area. Notice that when the highlighted bar is on E5 the function target range is B5..D5, while when the highlighted bar is moved to E8 the function target range changes to B8..D8 which indicates that copying formulae with this method causes the 'relative' target range to be copied. Had the 'absolute' target range been copied instead, the result of the various summations would have been wrong.

15

Now complete the insertion of functions and formulae in the rest of the worksheet, noting that 'Total Cost' is the summation of rows 8 through 13, 'Profit' is the subtraction of 'Total Cost' from 'Consultancy', and that 'Cumulat' in row 19 refers to cumulative profit.

Having completed the above tasks, add another column to your worksheet to calculate (and place in column F) the average monthly values of earnings, costs, and profit, using the @AVG( ) function. The worksheet should look as follows:

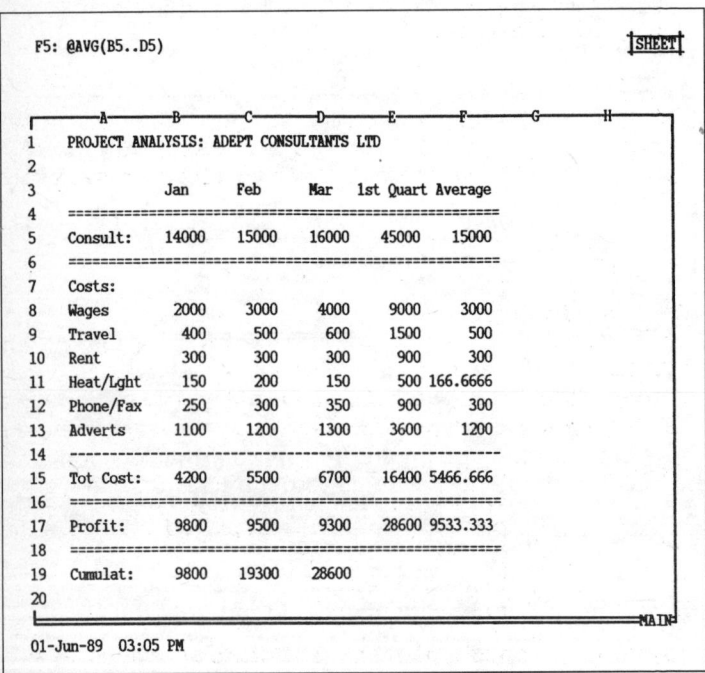

Formatting Numbers:
Note the contents of F11, F15 and F17, under the 'Average' column, are no longer whole numbers. Furthermore, the number of digits after the decimal point is variable and depends on the available space – the width of the appropriate field.

To make our present worksheet more presentable, we need to format specific cells so that we are in control of what is printed out. To format the contents of a numeric cell or block of cells, highlight the starting target cell (in our example, F5) and type {**Menu**} Format **F**ixed, and then press

16

\<Enter\>	to confirm the default selection of two decimal places.
.	to anchor beginning of target area
Down Arrow	to highlight target range (F5..F17 for this example)
\<Enter\>	to confirm target range.

It is possible that when numbers are formatted in this way, they might not fit into the default allocated space (width) of their cells. If that happens, you will know, as Symphony fills such cells with asterisks (*).

Changing the Default Width of Cells:

To change the width of columns (in order to accommodate either large numbers or numbers expressed in the form of currency, type {**Menu**} **W**idth **S**et and change the default value from 9 to, say, 12.

When the worksheet is 'Saved', this column width display format will be saved with it.

Changing Default Currency & Date Formats:

To change the default formats of currency and date from $ and MM-DD-YY to UK's £ and DD/MM/YY, type {**Services**} **C**onfiguration **O**ther **I**nternational **C**urrency, and backspace to delete the $ sign and type the £ to select UK currency, then press

\<Enter\>	to confirm selection
P	to select **P**refix so that the currency symbol prefixes numbers displayed in 'Currency' (£xxxxx.xx) format.
D	to select **D**ate
B	to select option **B**.

To make these options permanent, return to a previous menu by pressing **Q** (for **Q**uit), and then press

U	to select and execute **U**pdate
Q	to **Q**uit.

Printing a Worksheet:
To print a worksheet, make sure that the printer is switched on and that the highlighted bar is in the <Home> position and the worksheet mode is on 'SHEET'.

Now, type {**Services**} Print Settings Source Range, and press

.	to anchor range from Home (A1) position
Arrows	to move cell pointer to the bottom right-hand corner of the rectangle you wish to print
<Enter>	to confirm selection
Q	to select Quit
G	to select Go

which should start printing. It is, of course, assumed that you have configured your system to your printer. If you have not done this configuration (see next section) your printer might not respond to your print commands. On completion of the printout, press

Q	to select Quit

and return to the 'SHEET' mode.

A request to print again, will automatically remember the previous range. If you require a different range, then when the highlighted rectangular area appears on screen, as a result of previous print commands, cancel the current range by pressing the <Esc> key, then move the cell pointer to the required starting position (top left-hand corner) of target area, and press

.	to anchor top left hand corner of rectangle
Arrows	to move the cell pointer to the bottom right-hand corner of rectangle you require to print
<Enter>	to confirm selection.

Carry out the suggested formatting changes to column F of worksheet PROJECT2 and then arrange for the £ sign to prefix the consultancy entries in row 5. You will have to have changed the default 'Currency' format of your worksheet in order to do this successfully. Then, save the resultant worksheet as PROJECT3 and use your printer to print out the rectangle A1 to F20. Your printout should look as shown over the page.

If your worksheet is too wide for your printer, you might have to print it out in either condensed print or in two rectangular strips and glue them together.

```
        A        B        C        D        E        F        G
1   PROJECT ANALYSIS: ADEPT CONSULTANTS LTD
2      *
3                Jan      Feb      Mar    1st Quart   Average
4   ==========================================================
5   Consult:  £14,000  £15,000  £16,000  £45,000   £15,000.00
6   ==========================================================
7   Costs:
8   Wages       2000     3000     4000     9000      3000.00
9   Travel       400      500      600     1500       500.00
10  Rent         300      300      300      900       300.00
11  Heat/Lght    150      200      150      500       166.67
12  Phone/Fax    250      300      350      900       300.00
13  Adverts     1100     1200     1300     3600      1200.00
14  ----------------------------------------------------------
15  Tot Cost:   4200     5500     6700    16400      5466.67
16  ==========================================================
17  Profit:     9800     9500     9300    28600      9533.33
18  ==========================================================
19  Cumulat:    9800    19300    28600
20
                                                          MAIN
```

Printer Installation:

To install your printer you must return to the 'Symphony Access System' menu and choose the 'Install' option. This will cause a sub-menu to appear on the screen, as follows:

```
First-Time Installation
Change Selected Equipment
Advanced Options
Exit Install Program
```

with the first option highlighted. Use the Down Arrow key to move the highlighted bar to

```
Change Selected Equipment
```

and press <Enter>. This will cause a further sub-menu to appear on the screen, as follows:

```
Return to Main Menu
Screen Display
Text Printer(s)
Graphics Printer(s)
Communications Options
Save Changes
Exit Install Program
```

with the highlighted bar on the first option. Use the Down Arrow key to select

Text Printer(s)

which will display a list of printers. Select your printer with the use of the Arrow keys and press <Enter> to select it. Repeat the process for

Graphics Printer(s)

and then select option

Save Changes

pressing <Enter> to save changes into highlighted (LOTUS) driver set. Pressing <Enter> once more causes the program to ask for confirmation before leaving the 'Install' option.

WORKSHEET SKILLS & GRAPHS

We will now use the worksheet saved under PROJECT3 (see end of previous chapter) to show how we can add to it, rearrange information in it and freeze titles in order to make entries easier, before going on to discuss more advanced topics. If you haven't saved PROJECT3 on disc, it will be necessary for you to enter the information shown below into Symphony so that you can benefit from what is to be introduced at this point. Having done this, do save it under PROJECT3 before going on with the suggested alterations.

If you have saved PROJECT3, then load Symphony and when the mode indicator reads 'SHEET', type {**Services**} File Retrieve, and highlight PROJECT3. On pressing <Enter>, the worksheet is displayed on the screen as shown below.

```
         A        B        C        D        E          F           G
 1   PROJECT ANALYSIS: ADEPT CONSULTANTS LTD
 2
 3               Jan      Feb      Mar    1st Quart   Average
 4           ==========================================================
 5   Consult:  £14,000  £15,000  £16,000  £45,000   £15,000.00
 6           ==========================================================
 7   Costs:
 8   Wages      2000     3000     4000     9000      3000.00
 9   Travel      400      500      600     1500       500.00
10   Rent        300      300      300      900       300.00
11   Heat/Lght   150      200      150      500       166.67
12   Phone/Fax   250      300      350      900       300.00
13   Adverts    1100     1200     1300     3600      1200.00
14           ----------------------------------------------------------
15   Tot Cost:  4200     5500     6700    16400      5466.67
16           ==========================================================
17   Profit:    9800     9500     9300    28600      9533.33
18           ==========================================================
19   Cumulat:   9800    19300    28600
20
                                                              MAIN
```

What we would like to do now is to add some more information to the worksheet with the insertion of another quarter's figures in columns between E and F.

The {Menu} Insert Command:
To insert columns into a worksheet, move the highlighted bar to the column where insertion is to be made (in this case F1) and type {**Menu**} Insert Columns. Then use

21

| Right arrow | to highlight range F1..I1 |
| <Enter> | to confirm range selection and execute. |

On execution, empty cells are inserted into the worksheet in the requested range, and in this case, the column headed 'Average' now appears in column J.

We could now start entering information into the empty columns, but if we did this first, we would then have to first copy and then edit appropriately the various formulae used to calculate the various results for the first quarter.

An alternative way is to copy everything from the first quarter to the second and then only edit the actual numeric information within the various columns. We will choose this second method to achieve our goal. First highlight cell B3, type {**Menu**} **C**opy, and then use

Right arrow	to highlight columns B3..E3
.	to anchor top right-hand corner of rectangle
Down arrow	to highlight block of rows 3 to 20
<Enter>	to confirm selection
Right arrow	to highlight cell F3
<Enter>	to confirm selection and execute.

Now edit the copied headings 'Jan', 'Feb', 'Mar', and '1st Quart' to 'Apr', 'May', 'Jun', and '2nd Quart'.

Note that by the time the highlighted bar is moved to column I, the 'titles' in column A have scrolled to the left and are outside the viewing screen area. This will make editing of numeric information very difficult if we can't see what refers to what. Therefore, before we attempt any further editing, it would be a good idea to use the **T**itle command of Symphony to freeze the titles in column A of our present worksheet on the screen.

Freezing Titles on Screen:
To freeze column (or row) headings on a worksheet, move the cell pointer a cell to the right (or below) the column (or row) which you want to freeze, type {**Menu**} **S**etting **T**itles, and then press

| **B, V** or **H** | to select **B**oth, **V**ertical or **H**orizontal |

which automatically sets, either both the headings to the left and above, or just those to the left or above the cell pointer's current position.

Moving around the worksheet, leaves the headings frozen on the screen. Any attempt to enter the frozen area causes the speaker to bleep.

Now implement the above changes and alter the numeric information in your worksheet into that shown below.

	A	E	F	G	H	I	J	K
1		NALYSIS: ADEPT CONSULTANTS LTD						
2								
3		1st Quart	Apr	May	Jun	2nd Quart	Average	
4		===						
5	Consult:	£45,000	£15,500	£16,000	£16,500	£48,000	£15,500.00	
6		===						
7	Costs:							
8	Wages	9000	3500	4000	4500	12000	3000.00	
9	Travel	1500	500	550	580	1630	500.00	
10	Rent	900	300	300	300	900	300.00	
11	Heat/Lght	500	150	120	100	370	166.67	
12	Phone/Fax	900	300	350	400	1050	300.00	
13	Adverts	3600	1250	1300	1350	3900	1200.00	
14		---						
15	Tot Cost:	16400	6000	6620	7230	19850	5466.67	
16		===						
17	Profit:	28600	9500	9380	9270	28150	10033.33	
18		===						
19	Cumulat:		9500	18880	28150			
20								MAIN

If you examine this worksheet carefully, you will notice that two errors have occurred; one of these has to do with the average calculation in column J, while the other has to do with the accumulated values in the second quarter.

Non-Contiguous Address Range:
The calculations of average values in column J of the previous worksheet are wrong because the range values in the formula are still those entered for the first quarter only. To correct these, highlight cell J5 and edit the formula shown in the control panel from

@AVG(B5..D5)

to

@AVG(B5..D5,F5..H5)

23

which on pressing <Enter> changes the value shown in cell J5. Note the way the argument of the function is written when non-contiguous address ranges are involved. Here we have two contiguous address ranges B5..D5 and F5..H5 which we separate with a comma.

Now copy the formula to the J8..J13 cell range by highlighting cell J5 and typing {**Menu**} **C**opy, and then pressing

<Enter>	to accept range to copy from
Down Arrow	to select beginning of target area
.	to anchor beginning of target area
Down Arrow	to highlight target area
<Enter>	to confirm selection.

Now reformat the numeric information in J15 and J17 cells by highlighting each one in turn and typing {**Menu**} **F**ormat **C**urrency, and then pressing

<Enter>	to confirm default decimal places
<Enter>	to confirm default range.

Relative and Absolute Cell Addresses:
Entering a mathematical expression into Symphony, such as the formula in cell C19 which was

`+B19+C17`

causes the program to interpret it as 'add the contents of cell one column to the left of the current position, to the contents of cell two rows above the current position'. In this way, when the formula was later copied into cell address D19, the contents of the cell relative to the left position of D19 (i.e. C19) and the contents of the cell two rows above it (i.e. D17) were used, instead of the original cell addresses entered in C19. This is 'relative addressing'.

In the formula we want to include in cell E19, we want Symphony to interpret the cell addresses of the two specific cells mentioned in it as absolute. For example, writing

`+E5-E15`

in cell E19 will be interpreted as 'relative addresses', but

`+$E$5-$F$15`

is interpreted as 'absolute addresses'. The $ sign must prefix both the column reference and the row reference. Mixed cell addressing is permitted; as for example when a column address reference is needed to be taken as absolute, while a row address reference is needed to be taken as relative. In such a case, the column letter will have to be prefixed by the $ sign.

Now type into cell E19 both versions of the formula; relative addressing first and then absolute addressing and note the difference. Finally, correct the formula in cell F19 in order to obtain the correct results shown overleaf.

To make life easier, Symphony has an {Abs} key (F3) which automatically puts the two '$' signs in a cell address when it is pressed in the 'POINT' mode.

The {Menu} Move Command:
In order to improve the printed output of the particular example we have been using above, we would like to move the caption to somewhere in the middle of the worksheet so that it is centrally placed when we print it out. To do this, we must first unfreeze the titles in column A by typing {Menu} Setting Titles Clear, then move to cell A1 and move the caption by typing {Menu} Move, then pressing

<Enter>   to select default range to move
Right arrow   to select target range (say D1..D1)
<Enter>   to confirm target range and execute.

The final display of your work should correspond to the worksheet shown overleaf.

Now freeze again the titles in column A, press the <Home> key and save the resultant worksheet as PROJECT4.

PROJECT ANALYSIS: ADEPT CONSULTANTS LTD

	A	B	C	D	E	F	G	H	I	J
1										
2										
3			Jan	Feb	Mar	1st Quart	Apr	May	Jun	2nd Quart	Average
4			======	======	======	======	======	======	======	======	======
5	Consult:	£14,000	£15,000	£16,000	£45,000	£15,500	£16,000	£16,500	£48,000	£15,500.00
6		======	======	======	======	======	======	======	======	======
7	Costs:									
8	Wages	2000	3000	4000	9000	3500	4000	4500	12000	£3,500.00
9	Travel	400	500	600	1500	500	550	580	1630	£521.67
10	Rent	300	300	300	900	300	300	300	900	£300.00
11	Heat/Lght	150	200	150	500	150	120	100	370	£145.00
12	Phone/Fax	250	300	350	900	300	350	400	1050	£325.00
13	Adverts	1100	1200	1300	3600	1250	1300	1350	3900	£1,250.00
14		------	------	------	------	------	------	------	------	------
15	Tot Cost:	4200	5500	6700	16400	6000	6620	7230	19850	£6,041.67
16		======	======	======	======	======	======	======	======	======
17	Profit:	9800	9500	9300	28600	9500	9380	9270	28150	£9,458.33
18		======	======	======	======	======	======	======	======	======
19	Cumulat:	9800	19300	28600	28600	38100	47480	56750		
20										

Adding Graphs to a Worksheet:

Symphony allows you to represent information in graphical form which makes data more accessible to non-Symphony users who might not be familiar with the spreadsheet format. In any case, the well known saying 'a picture is worth a thousand words', applies equally well to graphs and figures.

Symphony allows six different types of graphs to be drawn, each illustrating up to six separate ranges of data. These graphs can display dots, lines or bars, and you can add to them titles, legends, labels, and a grid. These graphs (you can have several per worksheet) can be displayed on the screen or can be saved separately on disc so that they can be sent to the printer later. The types of graphs available are:

Line	for connecting data points
Bar	for comparing differences in data
Stacked-Bar	for comparing cumulative data
XY	for X and Y relationships when both scales are numeric
Pie	for comparing parts with the whole
High-Low-Close-Open	for showing stock activity trends.

Graphs can be displayed quite easily, once the preliminary definition of data has been made, and the graph type selected, simply by pressing **P** (for **P**review). As graphs are dynamic, any changes made to the data on the worksheet are automatically reflected on the already defined graphs.

In order to illustrate some of the graphing capabilities of Symphony, we will now plot the income from consultancies graph for the PROJECT4 worksheet. First we need to define the type of graph to be displayed followed by the range of the data we want to graph. However, the specified range of data to be graphed must be contiguous for each graph. But in our example, the range of data is split into two areas; Jan-Mar (occupying cell positions B3..D3), and Apr-Jun (occupying cell positions F3..H3), with the corresponding income values in cells B5..D5 and F5..H5. Thus, to create an appropriate contiguous data range, we must first replicate the labels and values of these two range areas in another area of the worksheet (say, beginning in cell B21 for the actual month labels and B22 for the values of the corresponding income).

Before you start, however, consider what will happen if you used the **C**opy command for this replication. As these cells contain formulae, using the **C**opy command would cause the relative cell addresses to adjust to the new locations and each formula would then recalculate a new value for each cell which would give wrong results.

The {Menu} Range Values Command:

The {Menu} Range Values command copies only the value in a cell and not the underlying formula which calculated this value. To do this, make sure that PROJECT4 is your current worksheet and that the mode indicator is on 'SHEET', type {Menu} Range Values, and then press

Arrows	to highlight start of range (Jan in this case)
.	to anchor beginning of range
Arrows	to highlight entire range (Jan to Mar)
\<Enter\>	to confirm range selection, at which point you'll be asked to enter the range to copy to
Arrows	to highlight beginning of area to copy data range to (B21 in this case)
\<Enter\>	to confirm and execute the copy of data.

Now repeat the same procedure for labels Apr-Jun, but copy them into E21 to form a contiguous data range. Then do the same with the consultancy values, placing them in adjacent columns in the row below the months (starting in cell B22). Finally, clear the Title protection and add labels for 'Months' and 'Income' in cells A21 and A22, as shown below.

	A	B	C	D	E	F	G	H
3		Jan	Feb	Mar	1st Quart	Apr	May	Jun
4	===
5	Consult:	£14,000	£15,000	£16,000	£45,000	£15,500	£16,000	£16,500
6	===
7	Costs:
8	Wages	2000	3000	4000	9000	3500	4000	4500
9	Travel	400	500	600	1500	500	550	580
10	Rent	300	300	300	900	300	300	300
11	Heat/Lght	150	200	150	500	150	120	100
12	Phone/Fax	250	300	350	900	300	350	400
13	Adverts	1100	1200	1300	3600	1250	1300	1350
14	---
15	Tot Cost:	4200	5500	6700	16400	6000	6620	7230
16	===
17	Profit:	9800	9500	9300	28600	9500	9380	9270
18	===
19	Cumulat:	9800	19300	28600	28600	38100	47480	56750
20	
21	Months:	Jan	Feb	Mar	Apr	May	Jun
22	Income:	£14,000	£15,000	£16,000	£15,500	£16,000	£16,500

MAIN

28

The {Menu} Graph Command:
We can now proceed with the definition of the type of graph to be drawn. To do this, make sure that the mode indicator is on 'SHEET' and type {**Menu**} **G**raph **1**st-Settings **T**ype **L**ine **R**ange.

The Graph menu then reappears so that you can first select the **X** (horizontal) range, and then up to 6 vertical ranges (**A** though **F**) in a single graph. In this case we only need to select one vertical range as we are dealing with the income from consultancies only. Thus, first define the X range by pressing

X	to select the **X**-range
Arrows	to highlight the beginning of the range
.	to anchor the beginning of the X range
Arrows	to highlight entire range (in this case B21..G21)
<Enter>	to confirm range selection
A	to select the first range
Arrows	to highlight beginning of first range
.	to anchor the beginning of the A range
Arrows	to highlight entire range (in this case B22..G22)
<Enter>	to confirm range selection
Q	to select **Q**uit
Q	to select **Q**uit
P	to select **P**review

At this point, your screen should clear and a line graph, as shown overleaf, should appear on it. Should your computer bleep instead, then you must have made a mistake when defining either the type of graph or the data ranges. If that happens, then type **1**st-Settings **N**ame **R**eset to reset the settings and start again. If you don't use Reset you will find that Symphony remembers the previously defined range settings, which might be rather useful to you if you are defining another graph type which uses the same range settings.

Once the correct graph has been successfully displayed on screen, you can **N**ame it for future use. To **N**ame a graph, use the {**Menu**} **G**raph **1**st-Settings **N**ame command which will display the **N**ame menu. This is a list of options which lets you **U**se, **C**reate, **D**elete, etc., a graph name. Select **C**reate, which will prompt you for a graph name. In this case type in the name INCOME and press <Enter>.

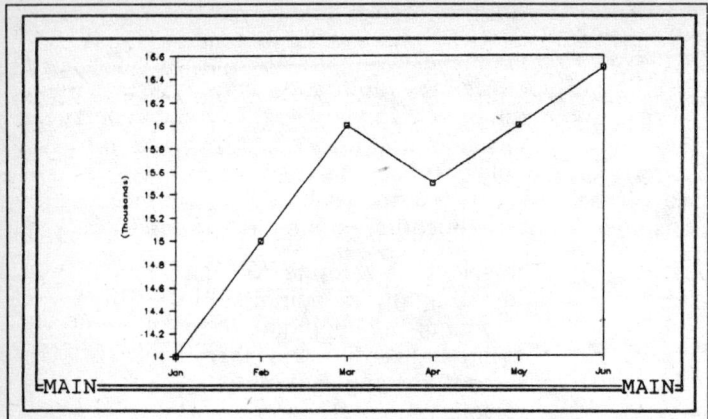

The named settings of the last graph remain those current, and when you select new settings, the current ones are presented as default so that you can reuse as many of these as you like. This reduces the time required to define new settings for a graph that happens to be rather similar to one you have already defined.

Now save the worksheet under the filename PROJECT5. This will ensure that your named graphs are also saved under the worksheet name. You can save as many separate graphs with the same worksheet filename as you like, provided you gave each one a different 'name', using the {**Menu**} **G**raph **1**st-Settings **N**ame **C**reate command.

Note: The {**Menu**} **G**raph **1**st-Settings **N**ame **C**reate command is different from the {**Menu**} **G**raph **I**mage-Save command. {**Menu**} **G**raph **I**mage-Save creates a separate file of the current graph on the data disc so that it can be printed with the Lotus **PrintGraph** program which is one of the options available in the 'Symphony Access System'.

Legends and Titles:
There are several options within the {**Menu**} **G**raph **1**st-Settings menu which allow you to add information to your graph.

The {**Menu**} **G**raph **1**st-Settings **L**egend selection, allows you to specify the wording of a legend which appears on the X-axis of your graph. In the case of our example, this was not required as the X-axis range itself was descriptive. Legends are not relevant to pie charts.

The {**Menu**} **G**raph 2nd-Settings **T**itles selection allows you to add titles to the whole graph, or add annotation to the X and Y axes by choosing appropriate options from the displayed list. To add a title to the previous example, use the {**Menu**} **G**raph 2nd-Settings **T**itles **F**irst option. To annotate the Y axis use {**Menu**} **G**raph 2nd-Settings **T**itles **Y**-axis and type 'Income' followed by <Enter>.

As an exercise, define graph settings for a new bar-type graph which deals with the monthly 'Costs' of Adept Consultants. As there are six different costs, you must define Data Ranges **A** to **F** inclusive, so that 6 different bars (corresponding to the six different costs) can be plotted for each month. Annotate and give a Title to your graph, as well as a Legend to mark different crosshatching patterns which represent the different costs. The legends describing these costs must be as short as possible (with six costs use only a single letter), if the printout on paper is to be correct. Don't forget to use the {**Menu**} **G**raph 1st-Settings **N**ame **C**reate command to make this graph current, and named 'COSTS'. The completed graph should look as shown below.

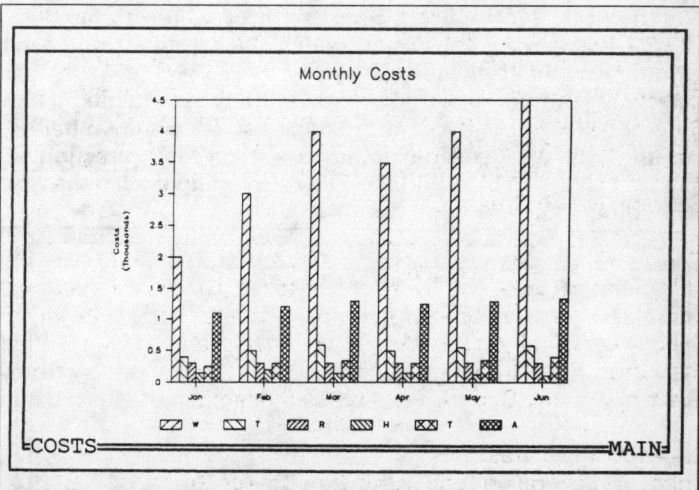

After viewing the barchart, use the {**Menu**} **G**raph **I**mage-Save command to save a .PIC file of this barchart for possible later use with the **PrintGraph** option of Symphony. Give this graph the name COSTS. The extension .PIC will be added automatically. Finally, save the worksheet with graphs by saving the worksheet under the filename PROJECT6.

31

As a second example, use the 'Average' values of the costs from your worksheet to plot a pie chart. Again define the new graph type as 'Pie' and then set the **X** range to the labels describing the costs (cells A8..A13). Now set the **A** (first) range of data to the actual cost values (which are in cells J8..J13) and view the result. You will find that the different parts of the pie chart are all labeled with the words describing the various costs in the worksheet and that percentage values of each cost appear next to them.

Crosshatching Code Numbers:
We need to provide code numbers for crosshatching of the pie chart as Symphony does not automatically shade the slices of a pie chart. The allowable codes are in fact from 0 to 7, each resulting in a different crosshatching pattern. The codes must be inserted somewhere in the worksheet and the B (second) data range should be set to them.

One way of creating automatically the required codes is to use the {**Menu**} **R**ange **F**ill command which first asks for a range to be defined for data filling (in our case this should be K8..K13), and then asks for the **Start**, **Step** and **Stop** values of the data. Use 1, 1 and 6 for these and watch the specified range fill automatically with these numbers.

Viewing the pie chart now shows the crosshatching of its different slices obtainable with codes 1 to 6, as shown below, starting with Wages and going in a clockwise direction. A selected slice can be emphasized by exploding it from the rest by adding 100 to its code number.

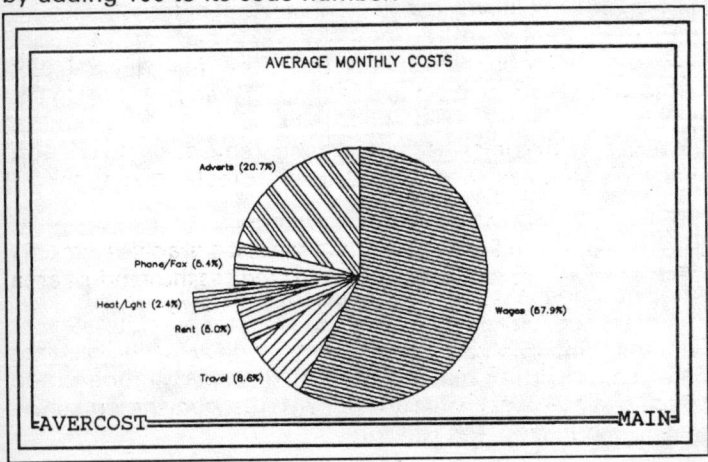

The available crosshatching patterns against their codes are shown below.

Make sure to save the worksheet again, with the above pie chart setting sheet named 'AVERCOST', so that we can refer to it later on.

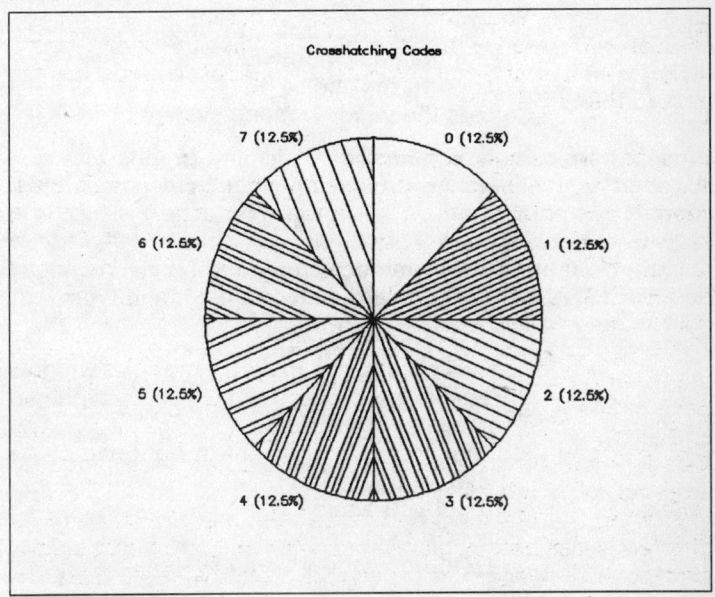

Crosshatching Codes

Graphics Windows:

Symphony also allows you to set up several different graphics windows, and by attaching graph settings to each, to have more than one graph current at any one time. By adjusting the window sizes several graphs can be displayed together on the screen.

If necessary retrieve the last worksheet saved, and to create a new window press {**Services**} **W**indow **C**reate, then type

PIC1   to name the new window
G   to select **G**raph and make it a graphics window
<Enter>   to identify the whole screen as the window area
Q   to **Q**uit the window menu system.

We now have a full screen graphics window with its name 'PIC1' shown in the right hand corner, displaying the graph whose settings sheet was current when the worksheet was last saved; in our case 'AVERCOST'.

Pressing the {Window} key (F6) will now toggle the screen between the spreadsheet and the pie chart, both of which are in different full sized windows.

Now press {Window} to return to the graphics window and use the {**Services**} **W**indow **L**ayout command, then press

Ctrl-Lt Arrow	5 times to reduce the size of the highlighted area to half a screen width
<Enter>	to confirm the choice
Q	to **Q**uit the window menu system.

If your hardware is configured to display graphs and text together you should now have on your screen the 'PIC1' graphics window sitting on top of the spreadsheet, which is in its own window named 'MAIN'.

Lets go one step further now and create another new window. Use the {**Services**} **W**indow **C**reate command, and type

PIC2	to name the new window
G	to select **G**raph and make it a graphics window
<Scroll Lock>	to enable movement of the whole highlight area across the screen
Ctrl-Rt Arrow	5 times to move highlight to right half of the screen
<Scroll Lock>	to toggle off again
<Enter>	to confirm selection
Q	to **Q**uit the window menu system.

The pie chart should now be duplicated on the screen which, as it stands, is not too useful. So, use the {**Menu**} **G**raph command to bring up the graphics menu and then press

A	to **A**ttach a graph to this graphics window. Highlight the 'COSTS' graph from the menu, and press
<Enter>	to confirm the selection.

The bar graph 'COSTS' should now be 'attached' to its own graphics window, named PIC2, and the screen should look like the figure overleaf.

We now have three windows in action, and pressing the {Window} key (F6) will make each one 'current' in turn. To work in a window, or change its settings, you must first make it current with this key. Finally, save your work under the filename PROJECT7.

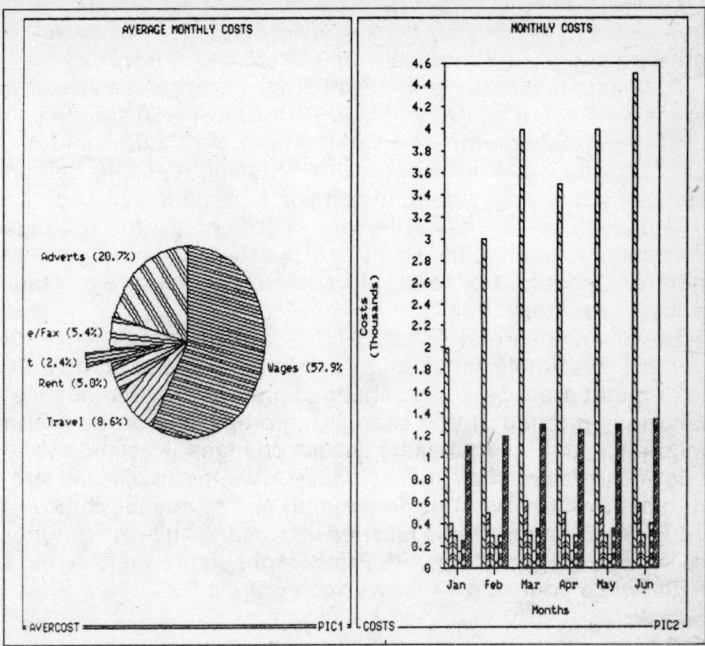

Using the PrintGraph Module:

If you are the first person to use the Lotus **PrintGraph** module you must implement it to accept the previously 'Saved' graphs which now have the extension .PIC. To do this, quit the worksheet and select **PrintGraph** from the 'Symphony Access System' and select **S**ettings **H**ardware **G**raphs-Directory and type.

`C:\SYMPH\DATA`

followed by <Enter>. This assumes that you have saved the .PIC files in the **DATA** sub-directory of the **SYMPH** directory on the C: drive. Then select **F**onts-Directory and type

`C:\SYMPH`

because the 'font' files are kept in the main Symphony directory. Now select **S**ettings **H**ardware **P**rinter to select the combination of printer and density of print required, then **Q**uit to return to the settings menu from where you should select **S**ave followed by **Q**uit.

35

From this point on, graphs can be printed on paper by selecting Image-Select and specifying the particular .PIC file you want to print on paper, and then selecting Go to begin printing.

Any changes made to the **PrintGraph** settings are effective immediately, but before you leave **PrintGraph** you should use the Settings Save command if you want to retain them for future use. However, before you make any changes to the default settings it might be a good idea if you first made a note of the original values. For example, you might choose the Settings command to change the size and proportion of a graph, select different fonts for text, and select colours if you have a colour printer or plotter.

However, be careful with such changes (don't save them until you are absolutely satisfied) as printing pie charts some time later might produce an egg-shapped graph after 10 minutes of laborious printing, if you change the proportion of the graph incorrectly. If you do make any such changes which you save and later discover they are not what you want, choose 'half size' graphs from the Settings Size menu, and save your choice. If you are not careful, you could end up wasting an awful number of hours experimenting with **PrintGraph**, due to the slowness with which your printer draws such graphs.

WORD PROCESSING

The Doc Environment:
Symphony comes equipped with a word processor almost as powerful as most "stand alone" versions. It has all the normal editing features, including the ability to insert, delete, erase, search for, replace, copy and move characters, lines and whole blocks of text. Symphony also allows you to enhance text and create bold, underlined, italic, superscript, subscript and other specially formatted text.

The word processor in Symphony 2.0 has been considerably improved compared to previous versions, especially its operating speed, and the addition of a range of short cut or "accelerator" keys.

Being an integrated package it is easy to embed part of a spreadsheet into a document, or send a document to a distant computer using the communications functions.

When Symphony is first loaded the window you see is the 'SHEET' window onto the worksheet. To use the word processing facilities the current window must be a 'DOC' window. To convert from a 'SHEET' to a 'DOC' window simply press the {Type} key (Alt-F10), the 'Type' menu appears at the top of the screen:

```
SHEET    DOC    GRAPH    FORM    COMM
```

Select 'DOC' from this menu to convert the current window to the 'DOC' environment in which all word processing is carried out.

The window now looks very different from that previously used (see diagram over the page). The familiar row numbers and column letters have been replaced by a top border line showing the default left and right margins, as well as the tab settings. The left of the control line shows the current cursor position as follows:

```
Line 1       Char 1       Page 1,6
```

"Line" represents which line of the document the cursor is placed on. "Char" shows which column across the page is current, and "Page" indicates the current document page number, followed by the line on that page on which the cursor is sitting. These settings will change automatically if the 'Print' settings are altered.

37

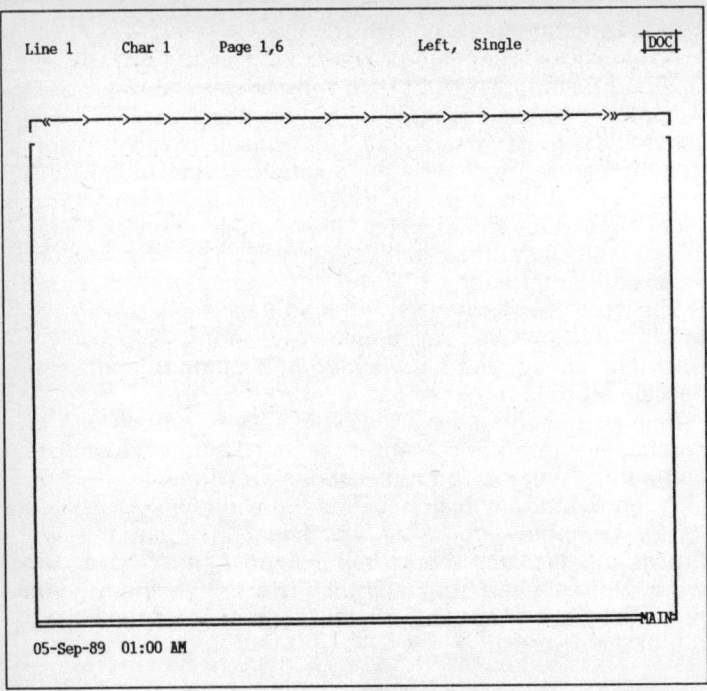

```
 Line 1      Char 1      Page 1,6           Left,  Single              ▐DOC▌
```

In the upper right corner of the screen are the words:

    Left, Single   DOC

"Left" indicates that the document will be left justified, or flush with the left hand margin. "Single" shows that it will be printed single spaced, and the 'DOC' which is in inverse video indicates that you are in the 'DOC' environment.

Note the special marker on both sides of the vertical border lines which indicate where page breaks will occur when the document is printed. Try pressing <PgDn> a few times to see where these occur and see the page indicator change to page 2.

Special Function Keys:
On the keyboard template provided with Symphony, the red function keys apply only to DOC windows as follows:

Keyname	Key	Function
{Justify}	F2	Justifies the margins of the current paragraph
{Where}	Alt-F2	Shows the curser's page and line position, depending on the current print settings
{Indent}	F3	Indents the whole paragraph
{Split}	Alt-F3	Splits a line of text at the cursor position
{Erase}	F4	Erases the highlighted block of text
{Centre}	Alt-F4	Centers a line of text between current left and right margins.

Before going any further enter the following letter, or something else if you prefer, to begin to get the feel of Symphony word processing.

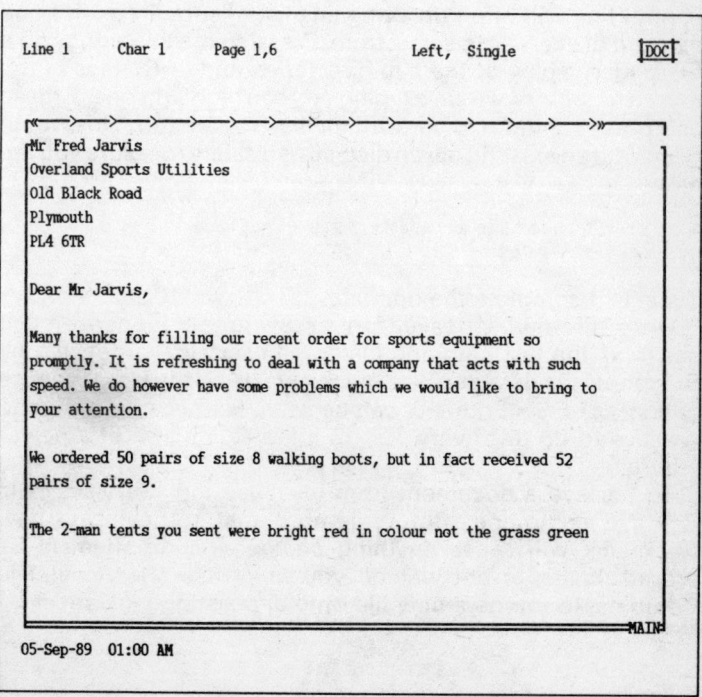

```
Line 1      Char 1      Page 1,6              Left, Single            DOC

  <-->-->-->-->-->-->-->-->-->-->-->-->->
 Mr Fred Jarvis
 Overland Sports Utilities
 Old Black Road
 Plymouth
 PL4 6TR

 Dear Mr Jarvis,

 Many thanks for filling our recent order for sports equipment so
 promptly. It is refreshing to deal with a company that acts with such
 speed. We do however have some problems which we would like to bring to
 your attention.

 We ordered 50 pairs of size 8 walking boots, but in fact received 52
 pairs of size 9.

 The 2-man tents you sent were bright red in colour not the grass green

                                                                    MAIN
 05-Sep-89  01:00 AM
```

You can start typing from the home position or press the Down Arrow key if you want to leave a blank line at the top. When typing the address, and at any other time you want to end a line or paragraph, just press <Enter>. For the rest of the letter the program will sort out line lengths automatically. This is known as word wrap. So you can just carry on typing.

Now is a good time to save the document, remember that all the current work will be lost if the computer is switched off for any reason, unless it has been saved to disk. The saving operation is the same as that used in the 'SHEET' environment, which is not surprising as with Symphony all of the different environments work in their own window types; but on the worksheet current in the computer memory. The save operation saves the whole worksheet to whichever disc and directory you specify.

Press {**Services**} File Save and if necessary use the <Esc> and <BkSp> keys to clear the default file saving path and edit to that required. For example to A:\FREDJ.WR1 to save to a floppy disk in the A: drive. Remember that pressing the {**Menu**} key (F10) while the blue FILES marker is showing on the right of the control line will bring up a one line list of sub-directories and existing file names to select from. Pressing it again brings up a full page display of the sub-directories and .WR1 files in the current directory. To save typing you can highlight one of these and press <Enter> to perform the save operation. This would overwrite an existing file on disc, so as a safety measure you are asked:

A file with that name already exists -- replace it?
No   Yes

Type Y to complete the operation.

Once a file has been saved further saving operations are much easier as the last path and file name used, are suggested by Symphony as defaults. So a quick save using the key sequence {**Services**} **F S** <Enter> **Y** can be used. For security it is good practice to do this every 10 - 15 minutes, in case of a power failure.

To retrieve a document from disc, use the {**Services**} File Retrieve command. But remember that retrieving a new worksheet will cause anything on the existing sheet to be erased. If this is not wanted you must use {**Services**} File Combine, to merge a new file onto an existing worksheet.

Document Editing:

It will not be long when using the word processor before you will need to edit your screen document. This could be to delete unwanted words, correct a mistake or to add extra text in the document. All these operations are very easy to carry out.

DELETION - For small deletions, such as letters or words, the easiest method is using the <Del> or <BkSp> keys.
With the <Del> key, position the cursor on the first letter to delete and press

<Del>   the letter is deleted and the following text moved one space to the left.

With the <BkSp> key, position the cursor immediately to the right of the character to be deleted and press

<BkSp>   the cursor moves one space to the left pulling the rest of the line with it and overwriting the character to be deleted.

Note that the difference between the two is that with <Del> the cursor does not move at all.

INSERTION - Word processing can be carried out in either of two modes, insert or overwrite. To change between these modes just toggle the <Ins> key. When in overwrite the status indicator 'Ovr' appears in the bottom right of the screen, and Symphony behaves like a typewriter overwriting all existing text in the path of the cursor. In the 'insert' mode any characters typed will be inserted at the cursor location and following text will be pushed to the right, and down, to make room.

To insert blank lines in your text ensure 'insert' is on, place the cursor at the beginning of the line where the blank is needed and press <Enter>. The cursor line will move down leaving a blank line. To remove the blank line position the cursor at its left end and press

<Del>

One of Symphony's function keys {Split} will also insert a blank line but regardless of the insert/overwrite mode. Place the cursor at the beginning of the line where the blank is required and press {Split} (Alt-F3). The text behind the cursor moves down leaving the cursor on the first character position of the new blank line.

EDITING BLOCKS - With larger scale editing, using the copy, move and erase operations, the text to be altered must be blocked before the operation can be carried out. These three functions are available when the {**Menu**} key (F10) is pressed:

```
Copy Move Erase Search Replace Justify Format Page
Line-marker Quit
```

Place the cursor on the first character to be copied, moved or erased, press {**Menu**} **C**opy (or **M**ove or **E**rase) and a prompt is displayed to the left of the control area, eg..

```
Copy  FROM what block? 11,1...11,1      or
Move  FROM what block? 11,1...11,1      or
Erase FROM what block? 11,1...11,1
```

The first number above is the start of the block location in terms of document line and column position. To define the block to be acted upon move the cursor to the last character of the block using the normal cursor movement keys, and the last number will alter as the cursor is moved. Then press <Enter> to start the operation.

   With copy and move the control line asks for the cursor location to copy, or move, the block to. With erase the operation is carried out.

   There is an important difference between the copy and move operations in Symphony's 'DOC' environment from that in 'SHEET'. In a 'SHEET' window anything copied or moved to a new location overwrites the existing material at that location. In a 'DOC' window, however, it is inserted in the existing text.

   Symphony 2.0 allows you to "paste" text that has previously been copied, moved or erased. The last block acted upon is stored on a "clipboard" and can be recalled at any location in the document by pressing the accelerator keys Ctrl-P. This facility can be useful if multiple copies of a section of text are required.

   Accelerator keys can also be used to initiate the operations of copying and moving, but not erasing, which has its own special key {Erase} (F4). These accelerator keys are:

Ctrl-C   to replace {**Menu**} **C**opy
Ctrl-M   to replace {**Menu**} **M**ove

In all these cases the blocking operations are carried out as before.

PAGE - To force a new page at any location in a document use either {**Menu**} **P**age, or the accelerator key Ctrl-N.

LINE-MARKER - It is possible to name individual lines, which with long documents can make navigation around the document easier. If you were producing a short book you could name the first line of every chapter - Chap1, Chap2 etc.. as follows:

Place cursor in the line to be named and use the {**Menu**} **L**ine-marker **A**ssign command. Then type the name, say "Chap1".

To rapidly locate that particular line from anywhere in the document type {Goto} Chap1 <Enter>, or, after {Goto}, if **F10** is pressed a list of named lines etc will be displayed, any one of which can then be highlighted.

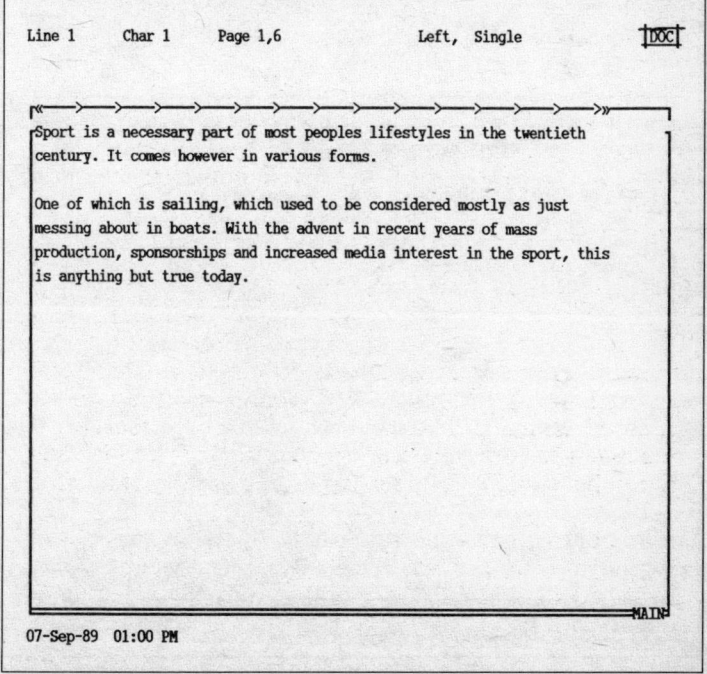

```
Line 1      Char 1      Page 1,6              Left, Single           DOC

 ┌«──>──>──>──>──>──>──>──>──>──>──>──>──>»─┐
 Sport is a necessary part of most peoples lifestyles in the twentieth
 century. It comes however in various forms.

 One of which is sailing, which used to be considered mostly as just
 messing about in boats. With the advent in recent years of mass
 production, sponsorships and increased media interest in the sport, this
 is anything but true today.




                                                                    MAIN
07-Sep-89  01:00 PM
```

INDENTING TEXT - A very useful and easy to use facility in the Symphony word processor is the {Indent} key (F3). This is used to indent the left margin temporarily, and works on the whole paragraph in which it is placed.

In Symphony a paragraph is ended by one of the following: a hard carriage return, a blank line, a format line or a non-text cell. The {Indent} key only works when placed on the first line of a paragraph.

Suppose you had written the text on the previous page, but decided the second paragraph would look better with a five character indent. Simply place the cursor on the first letter of the second paragraph, ensure you are in the insert mode, and press the space bar four times. Pressing {Insert} now will place an arrow in the fifth character position, and all the following text in the paragraph will be automatically indented to the right behind this marker.

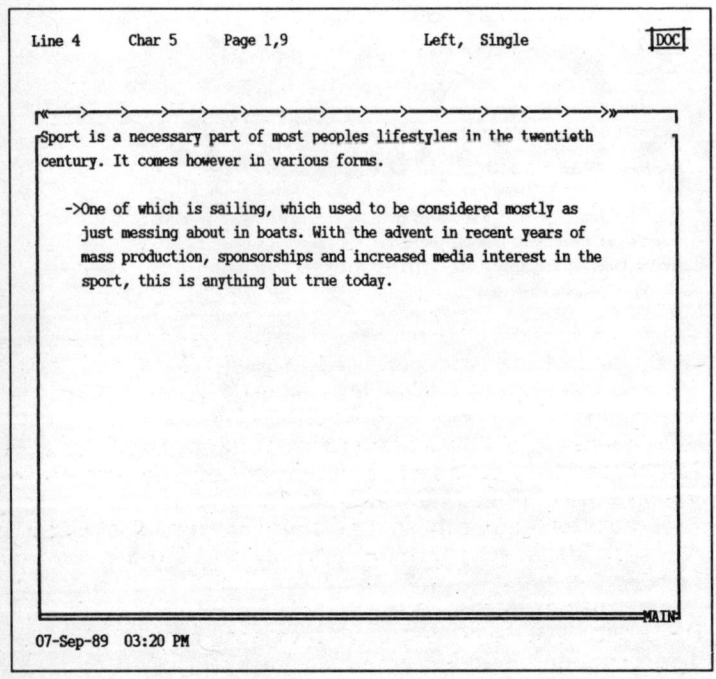

Print Attributes:

To enhance the printed document with such attributes as bold, struck-through or italic lettering, underlining, subscript, superscript and various combinations of these, type **Ctrl-B** to bring up the print attribute menu as follows:

```
B  I  U  +  -  X  1  2  3  4  5  6  7  8  9  S  Q
```

Where:

B	Bold
I	Italic
U	Underlined
+	Superscript
–	Subscript
X	Struck-through
0	Bold italic
1	Bold underlined
2	Bold italic underlined
3	Italic underlined
4	Bold superscript
5	Italic superscript
6	Bold subscript
7	Italic subscript
8	Bold italic subscript
9	Bold italic superscript
S	Start applying attributes to spaces
Q	Stop applying attributes to spaces

To enhance parts of previously entered text place the cursor on the first character to be altered and press **Ctrl-B**, then select the attribute from the above list, this changes the whole of the document from the cursor onwards - on a colour monitor the text changes colour from green to white. Move the cursor to the last character to be affected and press **Ctrl-E** to turn off the enhancement for all following text.

To help remember these accelerator keys the **B** of **Ctrl-B** is short for "Begin enhancement", and the **E** of **Ctrl-E** is short for "End enhancement".

When using underlined, the menu option **U** on its own results in words only being printed underlined, not the included spaces. To get continuous underlining, with the cursor on the first letter press **Ctrl-B U Ctrl-B S**.

You can also use the print enhancement features while typing text into a document. For example to enter a word in italics press **Ctrl-B I**, type the word required, and then end enhancement by pressing **Ctrl-E**.

Document Formatting:
The format of a Symphony document is controlled by a setting sheet, which can be accessed by using the {**Menu**} **F**ormat **S**ettings command. A typical document setting sheet is shown below. Any of the settings on this sheet can be changed by selecting the relevant menu item.

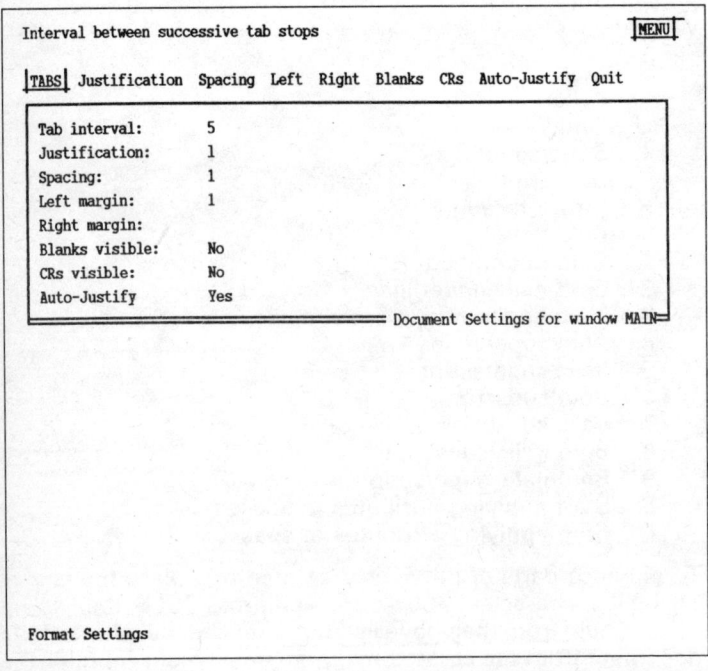

TAB INTERVAL - The default tab interval is 5. This number can be changed to any number between 1 and 240, to give regular tab spacing across the page. Irregular tab spacing requires the insertion of a format line, which is discussed later. If no tabs are required simply set the tab interval at a greater value than the page width.

JUSTIFICATION - Four types of justification are allowed in Symphony: left, even, centre and none. The default is "left" justification which produces a smooth left margin and a ragged right one. "Even" produces smooth left and right margins, but slightly irregular spacings between the words on a line. "Centre" justification makes each line of text central between the two margins, and the word-wrap facility is turned off. With justification turned off completely the text is left on the screen exactly as typed. <Enter> must be pressed at the end of each line to move down to the next. This setting can be useful for producing tables.

These settings are used in conjunction with the Auto-justify setting on the same sheet. With auto-justification turned on the document is readjusted automatically following every key stroke, or action. With it turned off each paragraph must be manually justified by pressing the {Justify} key (F2).

LEFT MARGIN - This controls the position of the left edge of text on the screen.

RIGHT MARGIN - This is a more complicated setting that can be set between 1 and 240, and works in conjunction with the margin settings on the print settings sheet. The default right margin is left blank, in which case it is determined by the size of window being used at the time. With a full screen window the default right margin will fall at character position 72.

SPACING - This determines the line spacing when the document is printed, but does not change the display on the screen. The default is single spacing, or text printed on every line. To print a double spaced document, use the {**Menu**} **F**ormat **S**ettings **S**pacing 2 command.

BLANKS VISIBLE - On this setting a dot is produced on the screen for each space in the document. This can be useful where very accurate spacing is required.

CRs VISIBLE - With this setting on **Y**es Symphony puts a triangular mark wherever a carriage return has been pressed in a document.

Format Lines:
All the settings above will apply to the whole document. To change any of the format settings for only part of a document format lines must be placed at the beginning, and end, of the text to be changed. In other words format lines can be embedded in a document, each one affecting the text until the next one.

To create a format line first put the cursor on the top line of the text to be reformatted and use the {**Menu**} **F**ormat **C**reate command. Press <Enter> to the question

`"Where should format line(s) be inserted"`

and a new format line is placed above the cursor position. As this new line is always exactly the same as the previous one (in this case the default format settings) a menu for changing the line settings is current at this stage. This allows you to change settings for tabs, margins, print spacing and justification. Make the changes you want and press Quit to return to normal mode. Note that all the document below the new format line is immediately formatted to the new settings (assuming that Auto-justify is set to Yes).

A new format line is now needed at the end of the text to be altered to return the remainder of the document to normal format. This is very easy. Place the cursor on the first line to be returned to default format and again use the {Menu} Format Create command. This time pressing Restore, on the menu will restore the default menu settings, and Quit will complete the operation.

The two commands on the Format Create menu we have not yet used are: Line-Marker and Use-Named. Pressing the former allows you to name individual format lines, so that you can place them again anywhere in the document with the Use-Named command.

We do not have the space here to discuss in detail how, but it is possible to create a library of format lines and setting sheets for use in any of your documents. However, this is beyond the scope of this book.

Accelerator Keys:

Several of these have been mentioned so far, the following is a complete list of 'short cut' keys which are available for document editing. The keyname in { } brackets is that used when referring to accelerator keys in macros.

Keyname	Key	Function
{Auto}	Ctrl-J	Toggles auto-justification on/off
{Begin}	Ctrl-B	Calls up print attribute menu
{Case}	Ctrl-X	Changes case of current character
{Copy}	Ctrl-C	Copies text
{Dleft}	Ctrl-T	Deletes text to start of line
{Dline}	Ctrl-D	Deletes current line
{Dright}	Ctrl-Y	Deletes text to end of line
{Dword}	Ctrl-BkSp	Deletes previous word
{Format}	Ctrl-F	Inserts format line
{Merge}	Ctrl-O	Inserts merge character
{Move}	Ctrl-M	Moves text
{NextPage}	Ctrl-PgDn	Move cursor to top of next page
{Page}	Ctrl-N	Inserts a new page break

{Paste}	Ctrl-P	Pastes text from clipboard
{Replace}	Ctrl-R	Replaces text with specified text
{Search}	Ctrl-S	Searches for specified text
{Stop}	Ctrl-E	Ends text attribute
{Toppage}	Ctrl-PgUp	Moves cursor to top of page.

Printing a Document:

To print a document in Symphony it must be on the worksheet currently in memory, as the programme will not print direct from a file. To print, say, a letter which you have typed on the current worksheet, and in a 'DOC' window, use the {**Services**} **P**rint command. This brings up a 'Print Settings' sheet and menu as shown below.

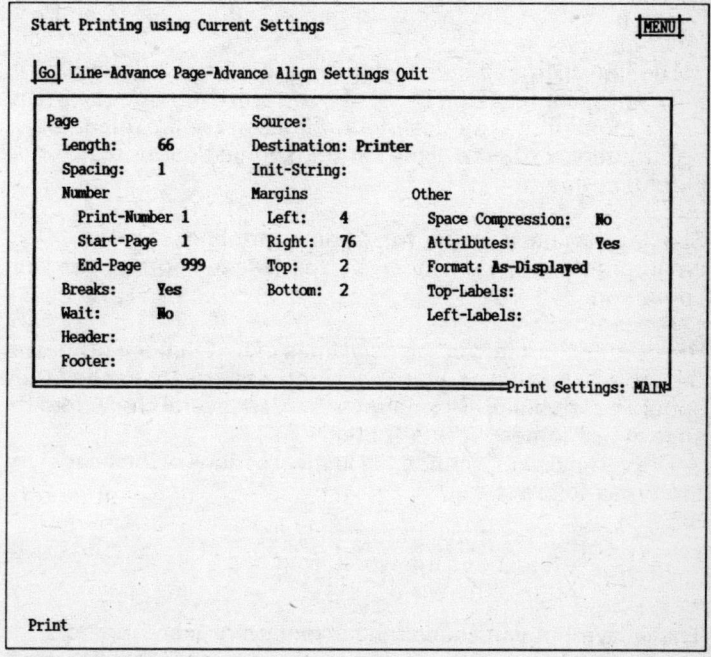

Switch your printer on, set the paper to the start of a page and press

A   to **A**lign the print head at the top of a page
G   to **G**o ahead with the printing.

This will print the whole of the current document using the settings on the sheet used, in our case 'MAIN' as shown in the bottom right corner. In some cases this may be perfectly acceptable, but by using the 'Print Settings' sheet you can vary the print output to almost whatever you want.

Line-Advance and Page-Advance simply allow you to move the print head down either one line, or one page, directly from the Symphony menu.

PRINT SETTINGS - To adjust a 'Print Settings' sheet use the {**Services**} **P**rint **S**ettings command. The following menu will appear above the current settings:

Page Source Destination Init-String Margins Other Name Quit

Name gives you the facility to name Setting Sheets and use different ones at will.

The first six menu items allow you to change the settings in different sections of the sheet. As you work through the menu items most of the top description lines are self explanatory.

Comments on some of the various setting options may prove helpful at this stage:

Spacing is used only for report printing; in the 'Doc' environment it is overridden by the {**Menu**} Format Spacing command.

Headers and Footers are special lines of text that are printed at the top and bottom of every page. If these are not needed they should be left blank. Symphony reserves several characters for special use in header and footer text.

The vertical bar "|" is used to justify sections of the header, or footer, as follows:

|Text   Right justifies the word 'Text'
Text| Left justifies the word 'Text'
|Text| Centres the word 'Text'.

The @ symbol will cause the current date to be printed.

Including the symbol # in a header or footer instructs Symphony to print the current page number. To try out a footer setting use the {**Services**} **P**rint **S**ettings **P**age **F**ooter command and type the following in the control line:

Confidential Report|Page -#-|@

The footer line is now included on the settings sheet. Set up your printer and press **Q**uit **Q**uit **A**lign **G**o.

If the main document text is less than a full page, the printer will have stopped in mid page, press Page-Advance and the footer will be printed as follows:

```
Confidential Report          Page -1-              14/09/89
```

Breaks - When this is set to No the printing of headers and footers will be disabled.

Init String - With most dot matrix printers you can control the typeface, size and spacing of the output by sending control codes to the printer. The {**Services**} **P**rint **S**ettings **I**nit-String command lets you specify a control sequence which will be sent to the printer each time the Go command is used.

Most control codes are given in printer manuals in several formats. Symphony needs the ASCII format, but entered in a specific way. To select double-strike printing with Epson compatible printers the control code is <ESC> G. In ASCII format this is 027 071. When used in Symphony a "\" is placed as a delimiter before each separate ASCII code, so the Symphony control code for double-strike would be **\027\071**.

Some codes need a 1 or 0 trailing character to turn a facility on or off, eg below, the NLQ code. This character is just added to the Init-String, which is why some of the codes below have four digits.

Some of the most often used Epson compatible control codes, in Symphony format, are:

Draft text	\027\1200
NLQ text	\027\1201
Compressed	\015
Expanded	\027\0871
Double Strike	\027\071
Italic	\027\052
Bold	\027\069

With your printer manual it should now be an easy task to select control codes and to utilise your printer to the full.

In practice the most commonly used codes are to generate Draft and NLQ text. When printing spreadsheets the code for compressed printing allows much larger sheets to fit on standard paper sizes.

DATABASE MANAGEMENT

A Symphony database is a worksheet which contains related information, such as 'Customer's Names', 'Consultancy Details', 'Invoice No.' etc. A phone book is a good example of a simple database, each entry, or **record**, consisting of name, address and phone number **fields**. In Symphony each record is entered as a worksheet row, with the fields of each record occupying corresponding columns.

Symphony has two ways of working with databases. The 'FORM' environment allows you to open a special type of window and attach a database entry form to it. All the data can be both entered into the database, and then manipulated, through this entry form.

The second method is to create and use a database solely in the 'SHEET' environment, without the use of an entry form. This second method will be familiar to LOTUS 1-2-3 users, and will be dealt with first.

Setting-up a Database:
In order to investigate the various database functions, such as sorting, searching, date calculations etc, we first need to setup a worksheet in a database format as shown on the next page. This consists of a row of field names, with records entered below them, and then the specification of a Database range.

Our database will be an 'Invoice Analysis' for a company called Adept Consultants and is designed and set out as shown, with the following field titles and field widths.

Start, in the 'SHEET' mode, with a fresh worksheet and use the {**Menu**} **W**idth **S**et command to change the width of the various columns to those given below, and then enter the abbreviated titles, as shown, with the last four centrally positioned. These widths were chosen so that the whole of the worksheet can be seen on the screen at once.

Column	Title	Width	Type
A	CUSTOMER'S NAME	19	Default
B	DETAILS	20	Default
C	INV.No	6	Fixed, 0 decimal
D	ISSUED	10	Date, type 4
E	PAID	4	Default
F	O/D	6	Fixed, 0 decimal
G	TOTAL	9	Currency, 2 decimal

```
A1: "          INVOICE ANALYSIS:    ADEPT CONSULTANTS LTD    AT              [SHEET]

      A              B                C    D      E   F        G
1           INVOICE ANALYSIS:    ADEPT CONSULTANTS LTD    AT      18/09/89
2     ================================================================
3
4   CUSTOMER'S NAME   DETAILS           INV.No  ISSUED  PAID O/D   TOTAL
5   VORTEX Co. Ltd    Wind Tunnel Tests  8901   4/6/89   N       £120.84
6   AVON Construction Adhesive Tests     8902   11/6/89  Y       £103.52
7   BARROWS Associates Tunnel Design Tests 8903 13/6/89  N        £99.32
8   STONEAGE Ltd      Carbon Dating Tests 8904  15/6/89  N        £55.98
9   PARKWAY Gravel    Material Size Tests 8905  20/6/89  N       £180.22
10  WESTWOOD Ltd      Load Bearing Tests  8906  20/6/89  N        £68.52
11  GLOWORM Ltd       Luminescence Tests  8907  20/6/89  N       £111.55
12  SILVERSMITH Co    X-Ray Diffract. Test 8908 26/6/89  Y       £123.45
13  WORMGLAZE Ltd     Heat Transfer Tests 8909  29/6/89  N        £35.87
14  EALING Engines·Dgn Vibration Tests    8910   2/7/89  N        £58.95
15  HIRE Service Equip Network Implement/n 8911  10/7/89  N       £290.00
16  EUROBASE Co. Ltd  Proj. Contr. Manag. 8912  18/7/89  N       £150.00
17  FREEMARKET Dealers Stock Control Pack. 8913 25/7/89  N       £560.00
18  OILRIG Construct. Metal Fatigue Tests 8914   3/8/89  N        £96.63
19  TIME & Motion Ltd Systems Analysis    8915  13/8/89  N       £120.35
20
                                                                    MAIN

18-Sep-89   10:31 AM
```

Use the {**Menu**} **F**ormat **F**ixed command to format columns C
and F to 0 (zero) decimal places, and then the {**Menu**} **F**ormat
Currency command to format column G to 2 decimal places,
before entering the information in the worksheet. Column F will
be calculated later using a formula which relies on information
in columns D and E. However, for the time being, leave this
column empty and, when you complete the other entries, save
the result under the filename INVOICE1.

The date in cell G1 is automatically updated to display the
current date. Type the formula '@Now' in the cell, and format it
using the command {**Menu**} **F**ormat **D**ate **4** <Enter>

Defining a Database:
Before being able to do any useful work with our database we
must first tell Symphony that this spreadsheet of data is in fact
to be a database. We do this by defining a Database Range and
creating a settings sheet as follows:

54

Place the cursor on cell A4, the first heading, and use the {**Menu**} **Q**uery **S**ettings **B**asic **D**atabase command to respectively activate the sheet menu, enter the sheet database options, enter database definitions, enter the basic ranges section of the database settings sheet, and specify a database range. Then press

.	to anchor the cursor
<End><Home>	to highlight the whole database block
<Enter>	to confirm the selection
Q	3 times to Quit the menu system.

Sorting a Database:
The records in our database are in the order in which they were entered, with the numbers in 'Inv.No' shown in ascending order. However, once records have been entered, we might find it easier to browse through the database if it were sorted in a different way; say in alphabetical order of 'Customer's Name'. Symphony has an easy to use sort function which can be accessed as follows:

Place the highlighted bar at the beginning of the range to be sorted (in this case A4), then use the {**Menu**} **Q**uery **S**ettings **S**ort-Keys **1**st-Key command to respectively activate the sheet menu, enter the sheet database options, enter database definitions, and select the Primary sort key. Then press

<Enter>	to confirm column **A** as the sort field
<Enter>	to confirm an **A**scending sort order
Q	to **Q**uit and backstep through the menu structure
R	to select **R**ecord-Sort option
A	to confirm that we want **A**ll the database to be sorted, with no deletion of duplicate entries
Q	To **Q**uit the menu system.

Issuing these commands will produce the display shown on the next page.

If you now decide to have a secondary sort field (say you want invoices for the same company to appear in ascending order of invoice number), its a simple matter to define a secondary sort range and resort the database. In fact three sort ranges are possible, which should be powerful enough for most purposes.

Now resort the database in ascending order of 'Inv.No' to return it to the original format.

```
A1: "          INVOICE ANALYSIS:   ADEPT CONSULTANTS LTD     AT          |SHEET|
```

```
         A              B            C      D    E    F      G
1              INVOICE ANALYSIS:    ADEPT CONSULTANTS LTD     AT      18/09/89
2       ==================================================================
3
4   CUSTOMER'S NAME    DETAILS           INV.No ISSUED PAID O/D   TOTAL
5   AVON Construction  Adhesive Tests     8902  11/6/89  Y        £103.52
6   BARROWS Associates Tunnel Design Tests 8903 13/6/89  N         £99.32
7   EALING Engines Dgn Vibration Tests    8910   2/7/89  N         £58.95
8   EUROBASE Co. Ltd   Proj. Contr. Manag. 8912 18/7/89  N        £150.00
9   FREEMARKET Dealers Stock Control Pack. 8913 25/7/89  N        £560.00
10  GLOWORM Ltd        Luminescence Tests  8907 20/6/89  N        £111.55
11  HIRE Service Equip Network Implement/n 8911 10/7/89  N        £290.00
12  OILRIG Construct.  Metal Fatigue Tests 8914  3/8/89  N         £96.63
13  PARKWAY Gravel     Material Size Tests 8905 20/6/89  N        £180.22
14  SILVERSMITH Co     X-Ray Diffract. Test 8908 26/6/89 Y        £123.45
15  STONEAGE Ltd       Carbon Dating Tests 8904 15/6/89  N         £55.98
16  TIME & Motion Ltd  Systems Analysis    8915 13/8/89  N        £120.35
17  VORTEX Co. Ltd     Wind Tunnel Tests   8901  4/6/89  N        £120.84
18  WESTWOOD Ltd       Load Bearing Tests  8906 20/6/89  N         £68.52
19  WORMGLAZE Ltd      Heat Transfer Tests 8909 29/6/89  N         £35.87
20
                                                                       MAIN
18-Sep-89  11:45 AM
```

Date Arithmetic:

There are several date functions which can be used in Symphony to carry out date calculations. For example, typing the function @DATE(89,4,18) - 18/4/89 backwards, works out the number of days since 31 December 1899, while typing @NOW (as in cell G1 of the worksheet), gives the number of days since the beginning of the century, but using the internal computer clock. Symphony uses such numbers to carry out mathematical operations using dates.

Another function, the @DATEVALUE, allows a date entered in the declared format of the spreadsheet (such as 18/4/89) to be used for calculations. Thus, typing

```
@NOW-@DATEVALUE("4/1/89") or
@NOW-@DATEVALUE(D5)
```

gives the difference in days (if the appropriate worksheet cell is formatted for integer numbers) between now and the mentioned date.

56

We will use these two functions to work out the number of overdue days for the unpaid invoices in our example, by typing in cell F5 the following formula:

```
@NOW-@DATEVALUE(D5)
```

However, before we proceed to copy the above formula to the rest of the F column of the database we should take into consideration the fact that, normally, such information would not be necessary if an invoice has already been paid. Therefore, we need to edit the formula to make the result conditional on non-payment of the issued invoice.

The @IF Function:
The @IF function allows comparison between two values with the use of special 'logical' operators. The logical operators we can use are listed below.

Logical operators
=	Equal to
<	Less than
>	Greater than
<=	Less than or Equal to
>=	Greater than or Equal to
<>	Not Equal to

The general format of the @IF function is as follows:

```
@IF(Comparison, Outcome-if-true, Outcome-if-false)
```

which contains three arguments separated by commas. The first argument is the logical comparison, the second is what should happen if the outcome of the logical comparison is 'true', while the third is what should happen if the outcome of the logical comparison is false.

Thus, we can incorporate an @IF function in the formula we entered in cell F5 to calculate the days overdue only if the invoice has not been paid, otherwise the string 'N/A' should be written into the appropriate cell. The test will be on the contents of the corresponding E column of a record, and will look for anything else but 'N'.

To edit the formula in cell F5, highlight the cell and press the {Edit} key (F2). Then press the <Home> cursor key to place the cursor at the beginning of the existing formula in the control area at the top of the worksheet and insert

```
@IF(E5="N",
```

then press the <End> cursor key to move the cursor to the end of the existing entry and add

,"N/A")

The edited formula in cell F5 should now correspond to that shown in the screen printout below. Now copy this formula to the rest of the range (F6..F19) and compare your results with those shown below.

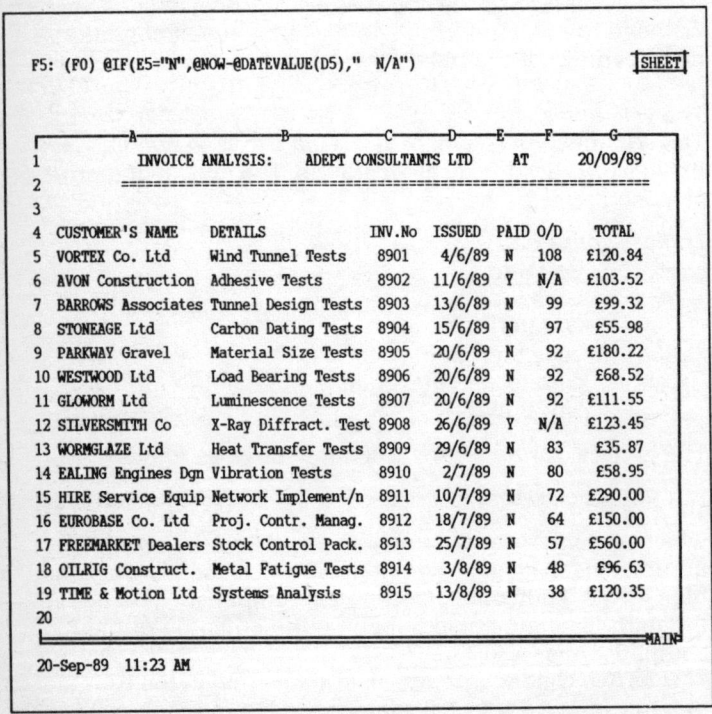

```
F5: (F0) @IF(E5="N",@NOW-@DATEVALUE(D5)," N/A")                    SHEET
```

	A	B	C	D	E	F	G
1	INVOICE ANALYSIS:	ADEPT CONSULTANTS LTD			AT		20/09/89
2	===						
3							
4	CUSTOMER'S NAME	DETAILS	INV.No	ISSUED	PAID	O/D	TOTAL
5	VORTEX Co. Ltd	Wind Tunnel Tests	8901	4/6/89	N	108	£120.84
6	AVON Construction	Adhesive Tests	8902	11/6/89	Y	N/A	£103.52
7	BARROWS Associates	Tunnel Design Tests	8903	13/6/89	N	99	£99.32
8	STONEAGE Ltd	Carbon Dating Tests	8904	15/6/89	N	97	£55.98
9	PARKWAY Gravel	Material Size Tests	8905	20/6/89	N	92	£180.22
10	WESTWOOD Ltd	Load Bearing Tests	8906	20/6/89	N	92	£68.52
11	GLOWORM Ltd	Luminescence Tests	8907	20/6/89	N	92	£111.55
12	SILVERSMITH Co	X-Ray Diffract. Test	8908	26/6/89	Y	N/A	£123.45
13	WORMGLAZE Ltd	Heat Transfer Tests	8909	29/6/89	N	83	£35.87
14	EALING Engines Dgn	Vibration Tests	8910	2/7/89	N	80	£58.95
15	HIRE Service Equip	Network Implement/n	8911	10/7/89	N	72	£290.00
16	EUROBASE Co. Ltd	Proj. Contr. Manag.	8912	18/7/89	N	64	£150.00
17	FREEMARKET Dealers	Stock Control Pack.	8913	25/7/89	N	57	£560.00
18	OILRIG Construct.	Metal Fatigue Tests	8914	3/8/89	N	48	£96.63
19	TIME & Motion Ltd	Systems Analysis	8915	13/8/89	N	38	£120.35
20							

```
                                                                  MAIN
20-Sep-89  11:23 AM
```

Your results will almost certainly differ from those above. The reason for this is, of course, that the @NOW function returns different numerical values when used on different dates. To get the same results as those shown, edit the formula in column F and replace the @NOW function with @DATEVALUE(G1) where G1 causes an 'absolute' reference to be made to the contents of cell G1. Now copy this edited formula to the rest of the F column range and change the contents of cell G1 to "20/9/89".

WARNING: It is important that you enter the date, in cells which will be used later for calculations, in the format specified as the default 'Date' format on the 'Configuration Settings Sheet'. It should be obvious that unless the @NOW function, which uses the specified internal format for date, is of the same type as the entered dates in other cells, to which you intend to apply 'date' arithmetic, then the result of such calculations will be incorrect.

If you have to change the default 'date' format, then use the command {**Services**} **C**onfiguration **O**ther **I**nternational **D**ate and choose the type preferred. Format 'B' (DD/MM/YY) is used in the examples shown. However, make quite sure that you use the **U**pdate command (one level back in the menu structure) to make your choice permanent. If you don't use the **U**pdate command, even if everything appears as it should be at the time, when you reload your worksheet later, the fields containing the results of 'date' calculations will be filled with ERR, because the worksheet will have reverted back to its previous default 'date' format.

After making the above suggested changes to your worksheet, save the result under the filename INVOICE2.

Frequency Distribution:

A frequency distribution of data allows us to find how many values in a specified range fall within specified numeric intervals (otherwise known as the bin range).

Thus, if we want to find out how many unpaid invoices exist in our database within 0-30, 31-40, 41-50, etc, days, then we need to specify the bin range in a column of the database and allocate another column to receive the frequency values. We choose to insert two columns between the existing F and G columns of the database by highlighting column G and using the {**Menu**} **I**nsert **C**olumn <Enter> command. Then, format the two new columns to the following:

Column	Title	Width	Type
G	BIN	5	Fixed, 0 decimals
H	FQ	4	Fixed, 0 decimals

Now enter the values you want to use as intervals for the calculation of the frequency distribution into the bin range column, in this case G5..G19, as shown in the worksheet output display on the next page.

To calculate the frequency distribution, highlight cell H5 and use the {**Menu**} **R**ange **D**istribution command, then press

Arrows	to highlight beginning of the data range (F5). You may need to select <Esc> <Home> to cancel the defaulted range
.	to anchor beginning of range
Down arrow	to highlight range (F5..F19)
<Enter>	to confirm highlighted area
Arrows	to highlight beginning of the bin range (G5)
.	to anchor beginning of range
Down arrow	to highlight range (G5..G19)
<Enter>	to confirm highlighted area.

The result of the frequency distribution is shown below.

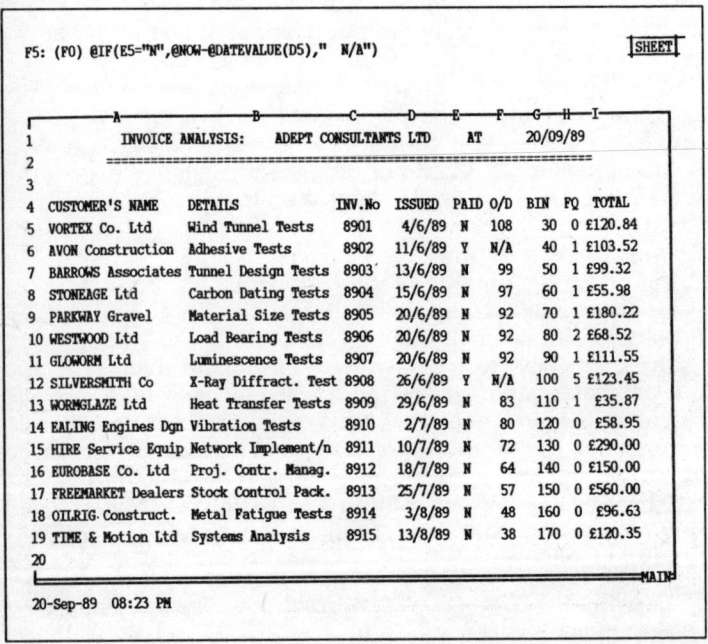

```
F5: (F0) @IF(E5="N",@NOW-@DATEVALUE(D5)," N/A")                    [SHEET]


        A              B              C        D    E    F   G   H   I
1       INVOICE ANALYSIS:    ADEPT CONSULTANTS LTD   AT      20/09/89
2  =================================================================
3
4  CUSTOMER'S NAME    DETAILS          INV.No  ISSUED  PAID O/D BIN FQ TOTAL
5  VORTEX Co. Ltd     Wind Tunnel Tests  8901   4/6/89  N   108  30 0 £120.84
6  AVON Construction  Adhesive Tests     8902  11/6/89  Y   N/A  40 1 £103.52
7  BARROWS Associates Tunnel Design Tests 8903 13/6/89  N    99  50 1 £99.32
8  STONEAGE Ltd       Carbon Dating Tests 8904 15/6/89  N    97  60 1 £55.98
9  PARKWAY Gravel     Material Size Tests 8905 20/6/89  N    92  70 1 £180.22
10 WESTWOOD Ltd       Load Bearing Tests 8906  20/6/89  N    92  80 2 £68.52
11 GLOWORM Ltd        Luminescence Tests 8907  20/6/89  N    92  90 1 £111.55
12 SILVERSMITH Co     X-Ray Diffract. Test 8908 26/6/89 Y   N/A 100 5 £123.45
13 WORMGLAZE Ltd      Heat Transfer Tests 8909 29/6/89  N    83 110 1 £35.87
14 EALING Engines Dgn Vibration Tests    8910   2/7/89  N    80 120 0 £58.95
15 HIRE Service Equip Network Implement/n 8911 10/7/89  N    72 130 0 £290.00
16 EUROBASE Co. Ltd   Proj. Contr. Manag. 8912 18/7/89  N    64 140 0 £150.00
17 FREEMARKET Dealers Stock Control Pack. 8913 25/7/89  N    57 150 0 £560.00
18 OILRIG. Construct. Metal Fatigue Tests 8914  3/8/89  N    48 160 0 £96.63
19 TIME & Motion Ltd  Systems Analysis   8915  13/8/89  N    38 170 0 £120.35
20
                                                                      MAIN
20-Sep-89  08:23 PM
```

From the frequency distribution display it can be seen that there are 0 invoices within the period 0-30 days, 1 invoice between the period 31-40 days, 1 between 41-50, 1 between 51-60, 1 between 51-60, etc..

Save this worksheet under the filename INVOICE3.

Searching a Database:

A 'SHEET' database can be searched for specific records that meet established criteria by the use of the {**Menu**} Query Find and {**Menu**} Query Extract commands. We will use the database of worksheet INVOICE3 to illustrate the method by searching with criteria relating to the frequency distribution of invoices.

Before we can find and/or extract information from a database we must set up two extra ranges in the worksheet, one for specifying the criteria for the search, and the other to specify the location for copying records extracted from the database. The latter will only be needed if you use the {**Menu**} Query Extract command.

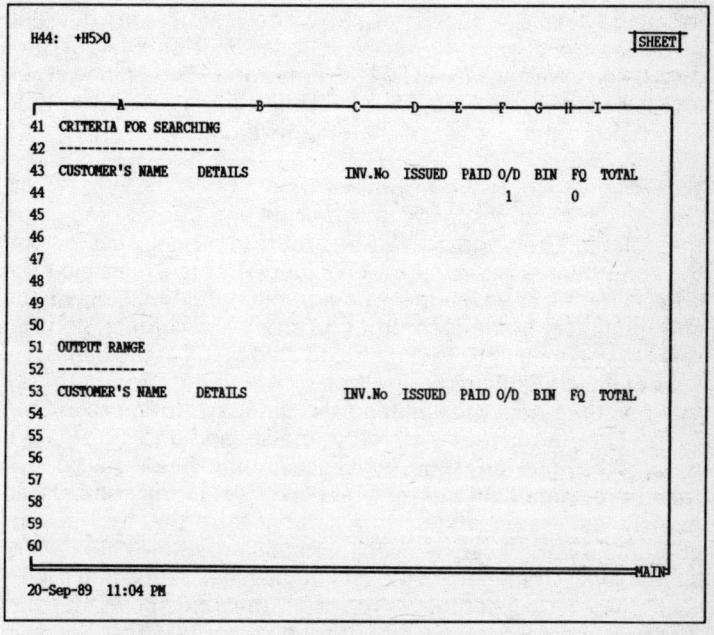

To do this, first copy the field names of the database (A4..I4) to an empty area of the worksheet, say, A43..I43 which will form the first line of the 'criteria range'. Label this area CRITERIA FOR SEARCHING in cell A41, as shown above, then setup the second area - the 'output range' - by again copying the field names to A53..I53 and labeling it as OUTPUT RANGE in cell A51.

CAUTION: In our case for simplicity we have chosen to put these ranges on the worksheet below the database. This has the advantage that all the column widths need no further adjustment. BUT in such a case care must be taken in the future not to overwrite the ranges if the database is added to.

In our case the database will not get larger, and it is easy to locate the range area by pressing <Home><PgDn><PgDn>. Alternatively, the range area could be protected in a separate window, which could then be jumped to with the {Window} key (F6).

We are now almost ready to search the database. However, before being able to do so, we need to enter into the row below the criteria field names (in our example, row 44) the criteria for the search. Assuming that we would like to search the database for all the details of our customers whose invoices are overdue by 80 or more days, but whose frequency distribution is greater than 0, then we type in cell F44 the criterion +F5>=80 and in cell H44 the criterion +H5>0, where F5 and H5 are the appropriate fields of the first record of the database data.

The {Menu} Query Find Command:
Finally, we need to specify the criterion and output ranges, on the database settings sheet. The criterion range must include the field names and at least one following row in which the criteria for the search appear (in our example A43..I44), via the {Menu} Query Settings command. Criteria may be included that refer to one field or to several (up to 256) fields of the database. Do not specify an empty line as part of the criterion range, as this has the effect of searching the database for *all* records.

The criteria must be entered in the second and subsequent rows of the criterion range, with each entered below the copy of the appropriate field name. A label or a value may be entered exactly as it appears in the database or the two special characters ? and * can be used to match any single character of a label or all characters to the end of the label. Preceding a label with a tilde (˜), causes the search of all labels except for that one. Thus, ˜Y* searches the database for all records with an entry in that field which does not begin with Y.

To search a database for values, either enter the value as the exact criterion or use a formula, such as +F5>=80 in which the logical operators (<, <=, >, >=, <>) can be used. The logical formula generates a value of 1 if the condition is TRUE or a value of 0 if the condition is FALSE. This value appears in the criterion range, unless the specific cell containing the formula is formatted to display formulae, by using the {**Menu**} Format Other Literal command. In which case the actual formula (or part thereof - depending on the width of the cell) will appear in the corresponding criterion cell.

Several criteria can be entered, either in the same row, if you want Symphony to search for records that match every criterion (i.e. criteria entered are linked with the logical AND), or one per row, if you want Symphony to search records that satisfy any of the criteria (i.e. criteria entered are linked with the logical OR). Compounded logical formulae can be used to create compound criteria that match more than one condition in the same field by using #AND#, #OR# or #NOT#. For example, had we typed the criterion in F44 as +F5>=80#AND#+F5<120 and erased that in H44 (unwanted criteria must be erased rather than over-typed with a space), we would retrieve the 8 records that were overdue by between 80 and 120 days.

To search the database for records which match the criteria discussed above, use the {**Menu**} Query Find command which causes Symphony to highlight the first record that matches the criteria which in this case is that of BARROWS Associates. Pressing the down arrow key finds the next record that matches the chosen criteria. If there are no more records (there should be 6 in all), Symphony bleeps. You can peruse through the chosen records backwards by pressing the up arrow key. Again, if there are no more records that match the chosen criteria, Symphony bleeps when the up arrow key is pressed.

The {**Menu**} Query Extract Command:

The {**Menu**} Query Extract command copies records that match the chosen criteria from the database to the output range of the worksheet. However, before trying this you must use the {**Menu**} Query Settings command to specify the output range into which data is to be copied.

It is imperative that the area below the output range is sufficiently long to accommodate all the extracted records. In our example, as we have chosen the output area to be in a part of the worksheet which has nothing below it, we can specify the output range as A53..I53. Specifying the output range by only the row of field names causes the entire area under these field names to be cleared before the extracted records are copied into the output range. So, beware!

If an output range of more than one row is specified, Symphony does not erase the contents of the worksheet below, but if such a multiple-row output range is not large enough to contain all the records that meet the criteria, an error message will be displayed.

Use the {**Menu**} **Q**uery **E**xtract command to extract the following records.

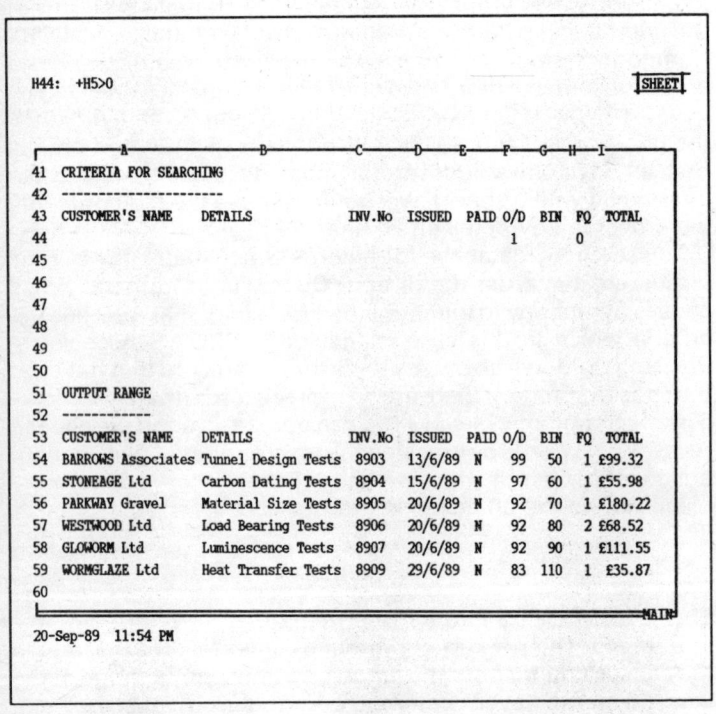

When the {**Menu**} **Q**uery **E**xtract command is being executed, the 'CALC' indicator appears in the lower right corner of the screen. After the selected records are copied into the output range, selecting **Q**uit causes the 'CALC' indicator to disappear and you are returned to the normal 'SHEET' mode.

Now save this worksheet under the filename INVOICE4.

The Symphony Entry Form:
When working in the 'FORM' environment you do not actually
see the database at all. It is still stored in exactly the same way
as described previously, but in 'FORM' you view the records one
at a time through an entry form. Hence of course the name! This
entry form has to be designed, and created, by you, with each
field on the form representing a field in the database. The form
itself is not used to store data, but is used as an "easy" way to
enter information into the database, and to manipulate it when it
is there.

With Version 2 of Symphony, form editing facilities were
incorporated, and the number of fields allowed in a database
was increased from 32 to 256. If this number is used, however,
in the 'FORM' environment all the fields must be on only one
entry form screen. If your databases are less ambitious it is
possible to have multiple entry forms on one worksheet. In fact
it is feasible to have several databases on the same worksheet,
each one with it's own named settings sheet.

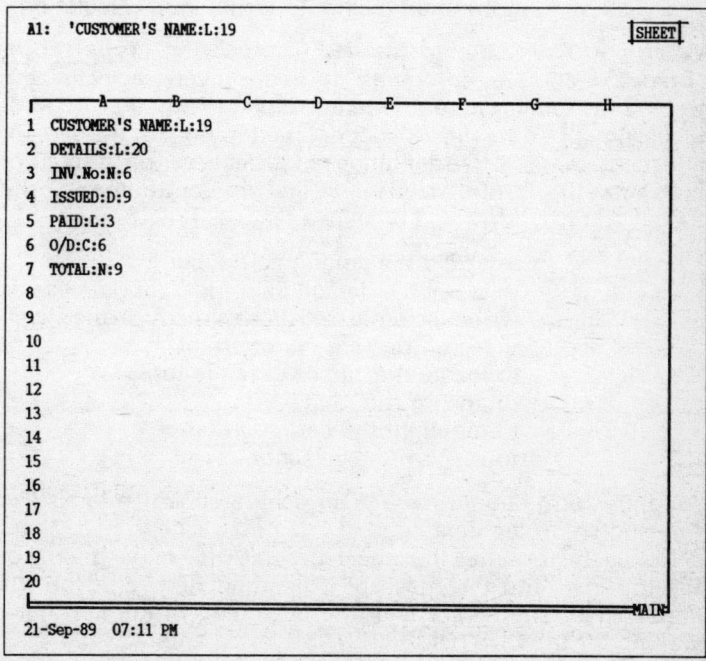

As usual the best way to demonstrate a new procedure is to work through an example. We will build up the same database example as before, but this time through an entry form.

Starting off with a clear worksheet in the 'SHEET' mode, we will first enter a list of the field names we want in the database, together with information on the type and length of each field. Enter the information from the screen printout on the previous page as shown. Type in cell A1

CUSTOMER'S NAME:L:19

The 'L' signifies that this will be a Label field holding alphanumeric data, while 19 is the field length required. Be sure to separate these items with a colon as shown above.

The possible entry form field types are:

L	Label
N	Number
D	Date
T	Time
C	Computed (will hold results of a calculation)

When you have entered the field list, use the {**Type**} **F**orm {**Menu**} **G**enerate command to respectively activate the Symphony environment menu, change to the 'FORM' environment - note the indicator at the top right of the screen, and the statement "(No definition range defined)" on the control line - show the 'FORM' menu for the first time, and automatically define an entry form and database ranges. Then press

<Enter>	to select the default field type
<Enter>	to select the default field width. In our case as we have nominated these already on the sheet, these entries are unimportant
<Home>	to locate the cursor at range top
.	to anchor the range
<End>Dn	to highlight the definition range
<Enter>	to confirm the selection.

An entry form should have been generated which looks like that shown on the next page.

Notice the form has the label **NEW RECORD** in the middle of the top line, and the message "Inserting Record 1" on the control line. The cursor is at the beginning of the first field, waiting for the CUSTOMER'S NAME to be entered.

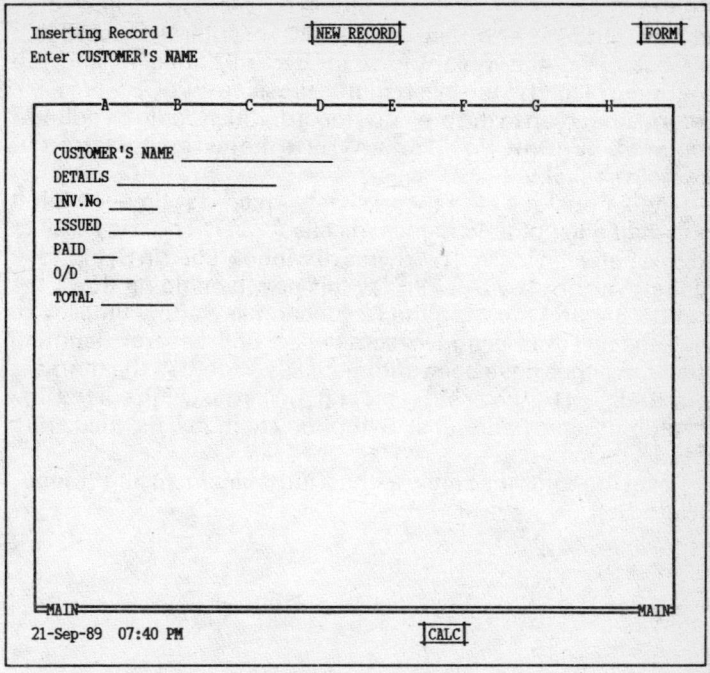

```
Inserting Record 1                  [NEW RECORD]                           [FORM]
Enter CUSTOMER'S NAME

        A       B       C       D       E       F       G       H

   CUSTOMER'S NAME _____
   DETAILS _____
   INV.No _____
   ISSUED _____
   PAID __
   O/D _____
   TOTAL _____




















  MAIN                                                              MAIN
  21-Sep-89  07:40 PM                         [CALC]
```

Enter the details for the first record "Vortex Co Ltd" from the previous listing. Press the {Help} key (F1) to see a screen of details which will help you to move around in the entry form. Note the other help screens available as shown on the bottom line:

    Moving Among Records
    Editing Records
    Deleting Records
    Help Index

Note that the entries in three of the entry fields do not look as could have been expected. When the date is typed in the format 20/9/89 it changes to 20-Sep-89 as the curser moves to the next field. The O/D field is ignored by the cursor, and the Total figure, in the last field rounds off to a whole number (121). All these points will be rectified when we complete entering the 'definition range' a little later on.

Complete entering the first record on the entry form, and when you are happy it is correct, press <Ins> to enter the record into the database. A new blank form for Record 2 appears, and you are again placed in the insert mode. Pressing <PgUp> now will return the screen to the previous record, which could be edited if required. <PgDn> would return you to the last empty form, but do not press it yet.

Let us now look at the worksheet, which last time we left it only had a list of field names in cells A1..A7. The easy way to toggle between the last two types of window used in Symphony is the {Switch} key (Alt-F9). Try this now by holding down the <Alt> key and pressing the **F9** function key a few times. The spreadsheet has changed somewhat, and several daunting looking ranges have been automatically added. At the moment these will not be too easy to understand as the widths of the first 7 columns have been set by Symphony to match the field entry widths specified.

Reset the columns below to the widths shown (using {**Menu**} **W**idth **S**et)

Column Width

D	10
E	8
F	9

You should now be able to see the contents of all the cells in the worksheet.

Database Ranges:

Five main ranges have been added to the worksheet. The settings for these are all stored on the Main Settings Sheet which can be accessed from the sheet with a {**Menu**} **Q**uery **S**ettings command, or from a 'FORM' window with the command {**Menu**} **S**ettings.

ENTRY RANGE - (A9-A15) - This contains the text that appears on an entry form. This range can be edited to improve the looks of a form, but it is strongly recommended that you save the worksheet before carrying out such an operation.

DEFINITION RANGE - (A18-H24) - This range forms the interface between the entry form and the database. It must contain eight columns which have the following functions:

| Name | Holds the record field names |
| Value | Holds the current record contents and format. |

	The current record is the one displayed on the entry form. Pressing <Ins> moves a new record from this column to the database range
Type	Shows the field type code and length
Default	Holds anything you want to be automatically entered in a particular field
Formula	Holds an optional instruction for the calculation of a field value
Validity	Stores optional checks to be made on the entry data
Input	Form entries are held here prior to any actions by the other columns, and before they are moved to the **value** column
Prompt	Holds optional messages to be shown on the form control panel. These can be edited.

REPORT RANGES - (A26-G27) - These are used when printing database reports.

CRITERION RANGE - (A29-G30) - Selection criteria are held here, as discussed earlier in the chapter.

DATABASE RANGE - (A34-G35) - This range holds the database, one record per row. It is automatically extended as new records are added through the entry form. BE CAREFUL if you add records in the 'SHEET' mode not to forget to extend this range manually, to incorporate the new records into the database.

Returning to our example, in the sheet mode still, reformat the following cells and ranges to ensure the database works correctly:

Range	New Format
B21	Date (D4)
B24	Currency (C2)
E23	Fixed (F0)
D27-D100	Date (D4)
G27-G100	Currency (C2)

Centre the labels in cells C34, D34, E34 and F34, and enter the formula below into cell E23

```
@IF(B22="N",@NOW-@DATEVALUE(B21),"  N/A")
```

As in the previous example this formula calculates the days overdue on unpaid invoices. Note that with an entry form it only needs placing in one cell in the definition range, whereas with a sheet database it needed placing in every cell in one column.

69

Now we have finished examining the definition range, therefore, reset the width of column F to 6.

Return to the entry form by pressing the {Switch} key (Alt-F9), and you will see that so far the changes we have made to the sheet have not altered the display in the entry form. However pressing the {Calc} key (F8) will recalculate the form, and the lower entries should appear correctly.

To build up the invoice database carry on entering the other 14 records through the entry form. When you have finished this you could browse through the records by using the <PgUp> and <PgDn> keys to step from one record to another, and the <Home> and <End> keys to jump to the first and last records respectively.

If you return to the spreadsheet your display should look something like that on the next page, except you probably will not be able to see the whole sheet on one screen. In this example the format of some of the entries was improved once the database had been built. For instance the labels in column E have all been centered.

Save the database to disk now with the name INVOICE5.

Editing an Entry Form:
If we wanted to continue building our database as in the previous example in the 'Sheet Query' section, we would now need to add two extra fields, called BIN and FQ, to the database. In the 'FORM' mode this is now very easy to do. Retrieve the worksheet INVOICE5, and make sure you are in the 'FORM' mode; if necessary by pressing the {Type} key (Alt-F10), and selecting 'FORM'. To edit the layout of the form you now have displayed, use the {**Menu**} **F**ield **I**nsert BIN command to respectively select the 'FORM' menu, enter the field editing menu, enable extra fields to be inserted, and type the new field name. Then press

<Enter>	to confirm the name selection
5	to select the length of field
<Enter>	to confirm the selection
Arrows	to locate the cursor at the start of the last existing field name (Total)
Y	to select **Y**es which confirms the operation.

Carry on and repeat this operation for the other field FQ, which would be a Numeric field of width 4. **Q**uit returns you to the normal entry form mode, and the new fields should now have been inserted towards the end of the form.

70

```
┌──A────────────B───────────C────────D─────E──────F───────G──────H─────I────────J─┐
 1 CUSTOMER'S NAME:L:19
 2 DETAILS:L:20
 3 INV.No:N:6
 4 ISSUED:D:9
 5 PAID:L:3
 6 O/D:C:6
 7 TOTAL:N:9
 8
 9 CUSTOMER'S NAME _____.
10 DETAILS _____
11 INV.No _____
12 ISSUED _____
13 PAID __
14 O/D _____
15 TOTAL _____
16
17 Name           Value          Type   Default Formula Validity Input    Prompt
18 CUSTOMER'S NAME HIRE Service Equip L:19                                 Enter CUSTOMER'S NAME
19 DETAILS        Network Implement/n L:20                                 Enter DETAILS
20 INV.No              8911 N:6                                            Enter INV.No
21 ISSUED         10/2/89 D:9                                              Enter ISSUED
22 PAID                N L:3                                               Enter PAID
23 O/D             219 C:6              219                                Enter O/D
24 TOTAL        £290.00 N:9                                               Enter TOTAL
25
26 CUSTOMER'S NAME DETAILS         INV.No ISSUED   PAID    O/D TOTAL
27 HIRE Service Equip Network Implement/n 8911 10-Feb-89  N      219    290
28
29 CUSTOMER'S NAME DETAILS         INV.No ISSUED   PAID    O/D TOTAL
30
31
32
33
34 CUSTOMER'S NAME DETAILS         INV.No ISSUED   PAID    O/D TOTAL
35 VORTEX Co. Ltd    Wind Tunnel Tests  8901  4/1/89   N     256  £120.84
36 AVON Construction Adhesive Tests     8902  11/1/89  Y     N/A  £103.52
37 BARROWS Associates Tunnel Design Tests 8903 13/1/89 N     247  £99.32
38 STONEAGE Ltd      Carbon Dating Tests 8904 15/1/89  N     245  £55.98
39 PARKWAY Gravel    Material Size Tests 8905 20/1/89  N     240  £180.22
40 WESTWOOD Ltd      Load Bearing Tests 8906  20/1/89  N     240  £68.52
41 GLOWORM Ltd       Luminescence Tests 8907  20/1/89  N     240  £111.55
42 SILVERSMITH Co    X-Ray Diffract. Test 8908 26/1/89 Y     N/A  £123.45
43 WORMGLAZE Ltd     Heat Transfer Tests 8909 29/1/89  N     231  £35.87
44 EALING Engines Dgn Vibration Tests   8910  2/2/89   N     227  £58.95
45 HIRE Service Equip Network Implement/n 8911 10/2/89 N     219  £290.00
46 EUROBASE Co. Ltd  Proj. Contr. Manag. 8912 18/2/89  N     211  £150.00
47 FREEMARKET Dealers Stock Control Pack. 8913 25/2/89 N     204  £560.00
48 OILRIG Construct. Metal Fatigue Tests 8914  3/3/89  N     198  £96.63
49 TIME & Motion Ltd Systems Analysis   8915  13/3/89  N     188  £120.35
└────────────────────────────────────────────────────────────────────────MAIN┘
```

If you now change to the 'SHEET' mode (the {Switch} key), you should see that the two new fields have been automatically entered in all the various ranges. The 'FORM' {Menu} Field command could also have been used to move field positions around the entry form, or to delete fields from the form and the database completely.

As an exercise you could if you wanted complete the INVOICE database to calculate the frequency distributions, as in the previous example. Remember to recalculate all the records, with the {Calc} key, once your formulae have been entered.

Using Selection Criteria:

There are several ways to 'browse' through a database using an entry form. The simplest is to move one record at a time with the <PgUp> and <PgDn> keys. If the database has more than a few records this method would obviously become very tedious.

A second method is to use the {Goto} key (F5). When in the 'FORM' mode, if the {Goto} key is pressed Symphony will ask

Go to which record?

If you can remember it, type in the record number you want and press <Enter>. The requested record will now be displayed.

With a big database you could not be expected to remember individual record numbers, so a third method, using selection criteria is available.

Before being able to use selection criteria we must first enter them in the criterion range of the database. In the 'FORM' mode this operation is carried out with the {Menu} Criteria command, which produces the sub-menu

Use   Ignore   Edit

If necessary load the worksheet INVOICE5 and as we have not used selection criteria before with this database we must press Edit to allow us to enter some. The 'CRIT' mode indicator will light up and the display line will show the message

Editing Criterion Record 1 of 1

Suppose we just want to review the customers who have paid their invoices. Move the cursor to the PAID field and type

Y <Enter>

To return to the 'FORM' mode press <PgUp>, but now only the records which match the criteria set will be displayed if we page through the database. In our case only 2.

Before we try another more complicated example we should first erase the existing criteria. Press {**Menu**} **C**riteria **E**dit to go into criteria edit mode, and press <Del> to erase the current settings. When entering a formula into a field on a criteria sheet a "?" must be used to refer to the cell address. Symphony automatically substitutes the sheet cell address in the formula.

Suppose we wanted to view all the records in our database that had invoices of over £100 outstanding for more than 90 days. Press {**Menu**} **C**riteria **E**dit, enter into the O/D field

+?>90

and into the TOTAL field

+?>100

<PgUp> will now let you browse through the selected records.

The command {**Menu**} **C**riteria **I**gnore will cause Symphony to operate in normal 'FORM' mode and not select any criteria that may be entered on the criteria sheets. To activate the current criteria settings again you use the {**Menu**} **C**riteria **U**se command.

Database Sorting in the 'FORM' Mode:
This operation is very similar to that in the 'SHEET' mode, as discussed in the previous section 'Sorting a database'. The first operation is to enter the sort keys in the settings sheet.

Let us sort the database on the worksheet INVOICE5 so that it is in alphabetical order of Customer's Names. In the 'FORM' mode use the {**Menu**} **S**ettings **S**ort-Keys **1**st-Key command to respectively activate the 'FORM' menu, enter database settings sheet, and select the Primary sort key. Then press

<Enter>	which causes the display to jump to the database sheet. Now highlight the column and confirm **A** as the sort field
<Enter>	to confirm an **A**scending sort order
Q	to **Q**uit and return to 'FORM' mode.

Finally, use the {**Menu**} **R**ecord-Sort **A**ll command to select the action required and confirm that we want the whole database to be sorted, with no deletion of duplicate entries.

The whole database should now be sorted alphabetically.

USING MACROS

A macro is a set of instructions made up of a sequence of keystrokes and commands that you would normally have typed onto the keyboard, but which you type instead into your worksheet as cell entries. After entering and naming a macro it can be invoked by simply typing its name. Thus, a macro is a list of commands which is used to perform a complete task and is used whenever we wish to save time in performing repetitive commands or make a worksheet easier to use.

Symphony also has a series of commands which can only be used in macros. This is the "Symphony Command Language". With this it is possible to create very sophisticated programs which can almost fully automate most spreadsheet operations. In the present volume, however, we will only be able to cover the basics of simple macro usage.

Creating a Simple Macro:

We will now use the worksheet saved under PROJECT3 (see the beginning of the "Worksheet Skills & Graphs chapter) to show how we can add macros to it, to perform 'what-if' type of projections by, say, increasing the 'Wages' bill by 15%.

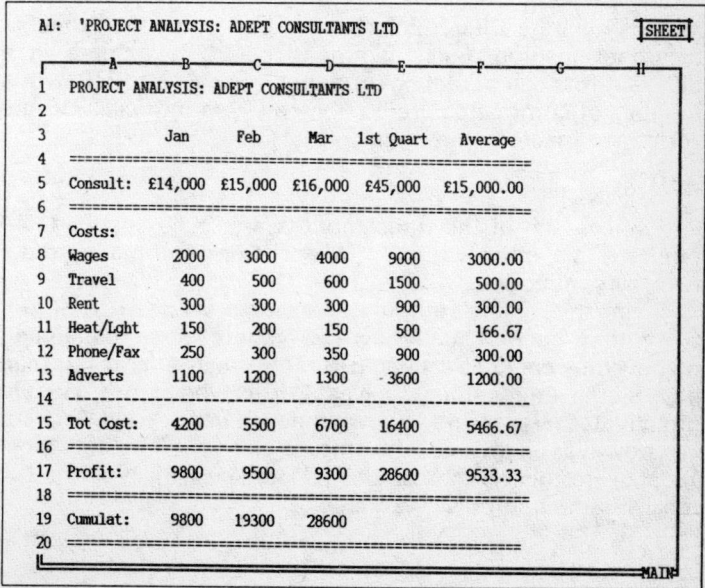

```
A1:   'PROJECT ANALYSIS: ADEPT CONSULTANTS LTD                    [SHEET]
      A       B       C       D        E        F       G      H
 1  PROJECT ANALYSIS: ADEPT CONSULTANTS LTD
 2
 3            Jan     Feb     Mar    1st Quart  Average
 4  ======================================================
 5  Consult: £14,000 £15,000 £16,000 £45,000  £15,000.00
 6  ======================================================
 7  Costs:
 8  Wages     2000    3000    4000    9000     3000.00
 9  Travel     400     500     600    1500      500.00
10  Rent       300     300     300     900      300.00
11  Heat/Lght  150     200     150     500      166.67
12  Phone/Fax  250     300     350     900      300.00
13  Adverts   1100    1200    1300    -3600    1200.00
14  ------------------------------------------------------
15  Tot Cost: 4200    5500    6700   16400     5466.67
16  ======================================================
17  Profit:   9800    9500    9300   28600     9533.33
18  ======================================================
19  Cumulat:  9800   19300   28600
20  ======================================================
                                                        MAIN
```

75

If you haven't saved PROJECT3 on disc, it will be necessary for you to enter the information shown above so that you can benefit from what is to be introduced. Having done this, save it under PROJECT3 before going on.

If you have saved PROJECT3, then enter Symphony and use the {**Services**} **F**ile **R**etrieve command to load the file. What should appear on screen is shown on the previous page.

What we would like to do now is to 'Edit' the entries under 'Wages' so that this part of the costs can be increased by 15%. One way of doing this would be to multiply the contents of each cell containing the 'wages' value by 1.15. To do this, we would start by 'editing' the contents of cell B8 by pressing F2 to 'Edit' the value in it by adding to the entry '*1.15' which has the effect of multiplying the contents of the cell by 1.15 which would increase its contents by 15%. We would then press 'Enter', press the Right arrow key to move to C8 and repeat the whole procedure. The exact steps, after highlighting cell B8, are:

Manual Procedure	Equivalent Macro Steps
Press F2 to 'Edit' cell	{EDIT}
Type '*1.15'	*1.15
<Enter>	~
Press Right arrow	{RIGHT}

Macros must be entered in an empty part of the worksheet in columnar fashion. Each command could be entered in a different row cell of that column, but it is easier to follow if a number of commands are combined. Type into cell H10 the combined macro commands

```
{EDIT}*1.15~{RIGHT}
```

and since each of the three months are to be changed, we replicate this entry, using the {**Menu**} **C**opy command, to the two rows immediately below H10.

Having thus entered the complete macro, we need to name it. Symphony macros usually have two types of names, depending on how they are to be activated. Simple macros, as in 1-2-3 can have single letter names, such as \A. This type of macro would be activated by pressing Alt-A whenever it was needed. A macro can however be given a full name, of up to 15 characters long. To activate this type press the {**User**} key (F7), type the full macro name and press <Enter>.

76

As we will stick to simple macros we will only use the former method, and will call our example macro \P (for percent). Enter \P into cell G10 and with the cursor in that cell type {**Menu**} **R**ange **N**ame **L**abels **R**ight <Enter>. The cell to the right of that highlighted is in this way given the name that is shown in the highlighted cell.

To test this has happened we could use the {Goto} key. Move to a section of the worksheet several screens away and press

{**Goto**}	to activate the **G**oto function and allow insertion of cell address to go to
F10	to display a list of ranges on the sheet
Arrows	to highlight \P
<Enter>	to confirm the selection.

The first cell of our macro should now be highlighted in the top left corner of the screen. This is a very useful way to 'jump' around a large worksheet. Your screen should now display the following information:

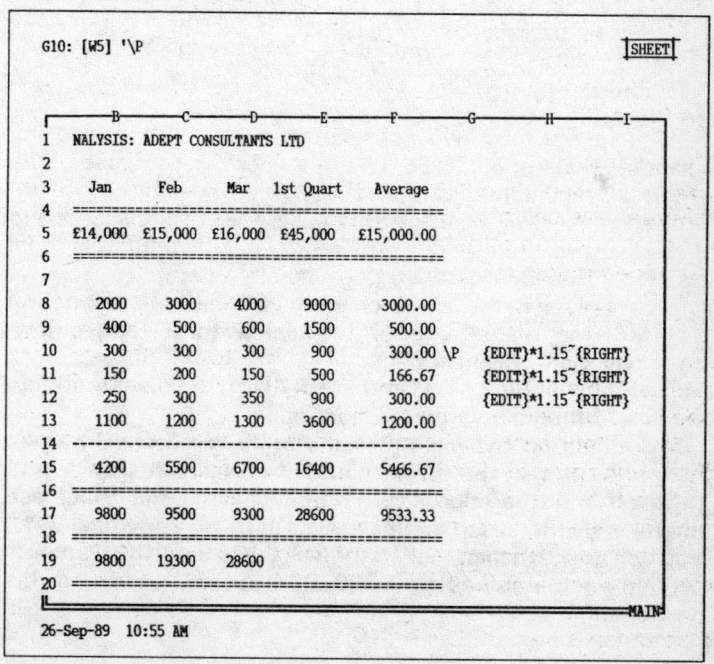

```
G10: [W5] '\P                                                    SHEET

        B        C        D        E        F        G        H        I
1   NALYSIS: ADEPT CONSULTANTS LTD
2
3     Jan      Feb      Mar    1st Quart  Average
4   ==================================================
5  £14,000  £15,000  £16,000  £45,000   £15,000.00
6   ==================================================
7
8    2000     3000     4000     9000     3000.00
9     400      500      600     1500      500.00
10    300      300      300      900      300.00 \P   {EDIT}*1.15~{RIGHT}
11    150      200      150      500      166.67       {EDIT}*1.15~{RIGHT}
12    250      300      350      900      300.00       {EDIT}*1.15~{RIGHT}
13   1100     1200     1300     3600     1200.00
14   --------------------------------------------------
15   4200     5500     6700    16400     5466.67
16   ==================================================
17   9800     9500     9300    28600     9533.33
18   ==================================================
19   9800    19300    28600
20   ==================================================
                                                              MAIN

26-Sep-89  10:55 AM
```

Before executing any macro, save your worksheet, in this case under the filename MACRO1. This is a simple precaution, if things go wrong your macro could damage your worksheet, and it is usually easier to reload the worksheet and edit the incorrect macro than to have to correct the worksheet!

To use this macro, highlight the first cell to be updated (in this case B8) and press **Alt-P**. Watch the changes that take place in cell range B8..D8 as a result of the three line macro (an empty row signifies the end of a macro), and beyond to F8, since the contents of cells E8 and F8 depend on the contents of cells B8..D8.

We could use the same macro to increase the other costs by a different percentage, by editing it, but this would be rather inefficient. A better method is to allocate a cell for the % increase, say cell H7, and edit the macro so that reference to that cell is made in absolute terms. For example, in cell G7, type

```
Incr
```

and in cell H7 type the actual % increase (in the previous case this would have been 1.15). Finally, edit the macro to:

```
{EDIT}*$H$7~{RIGHT}
```

copy it to the next two consecutive rows, and change the formulae that appear in B8..D13 to values, with the use of the {**Menu**} **R**ange **V**alue command. Use the arrow keys to highlight the range to copy from (in this case, B8..D13). On pressing 'Enter' you will be asked for the range to copy to (in this case, B8..D13). This is imperative because any attempt to increase costs of a given range for which this has already been done will give incorrect results, unless formulae in these ranges have been changed to values.

Finally, highlight cell B8 and press **Alt-P**. The display should change to that shown on the next page.

In both the last two examples, the width of column G was set to 5, in order that the macro could fit on the screen.

Now change the value in cell H7 to 1.20, to attempt to increase the recently increased values in B8..D8 by an additional 20%. You will notice in fact, that as soon as you change the contents of H7, the actual values in cells B8..D8 also change to reflect this new change.

```
B8: 2000*$H$7                                                      |SHEET|


     ──B────────C────────D────────E────────F────────G────────H────────────I─
  1  NALYSIS: ADEPT CONSULTANTS LTD
  2
  3    Jan      Feb      Mar   1st Quart    Average
  4  ================================================
  5  £14,000  £15,000  £16,000  £45,000   £15,000.00
  6  ================================================
  7                                              Incr=    1.15
  8    2300     3450     4600    10350      3450.00
  9     400      500      600     1500       500.00
 10     300      300      300      900       300.00  \P  {EDIT}*$H$7~{RIGHT}
 11     150      200      150      500       166.67      {EDIT}*$H$7~{RIGHT}
 12     250      300      350      900       300.00      {EDIT}*$H$7~{RIGHT}
 13    1100     1200     1300     3600      1200.00
 14  ------------------------------------------------
 15    4500     5950     7300    16400      5916.67
 16  ================================================
 17    9500     9050     8700    28600      9083.33
 18  ================================================
 19    9500    18550    27250
 20  ================================================
 ─                                                             ─────MAIN─
  26-Sep-89  11:25 AM
```

This, of course, will inevitably lead to errors, unless you
incorporate the command {**Menu**} **R**ange **V**alue within an
additional macro, which should be executed prior to any
attempt to change the contents of H7. Such a macro could
incorporate the following commands:

`'/RVB8..D13~B8..D13~`

Implement this in your current worksheet, name it **V** and save
the resulting worksheet under the name MACRO2.

Range Names:
It is a very good idea to give range names to appropriate cells,
so that reference to such cells can be made by range name
rather than discrete cell addressing. For example, the **V** macro
discussed earlier which had the commands

`'/RVB8..D13~B8..D13~`

could be rewritten to incorporate the range name 'Costs' as
follows:

79

`'/RVCosts˜Costs˜`

where 'Costs' was defined as the range name for the cell block B8..D13.

To name a block of cells by a range name, highlight the left top corner of the block and then use the {**Menu**} **R**ange **N**ame **C**reate command, give the name and highlight the block of cells you want to be referred to by that name.

Implement this in your current worksheet, and then save it under the name MACRO2, replacing the previously saved version. Note that we have placed both these macros (macro **P** and macro **V**) on specific row numbers of column H with a gap between them. This has been chosen intentionally, so as to allow room for future expansion of this example.

What you should have on your screen, is the following display:

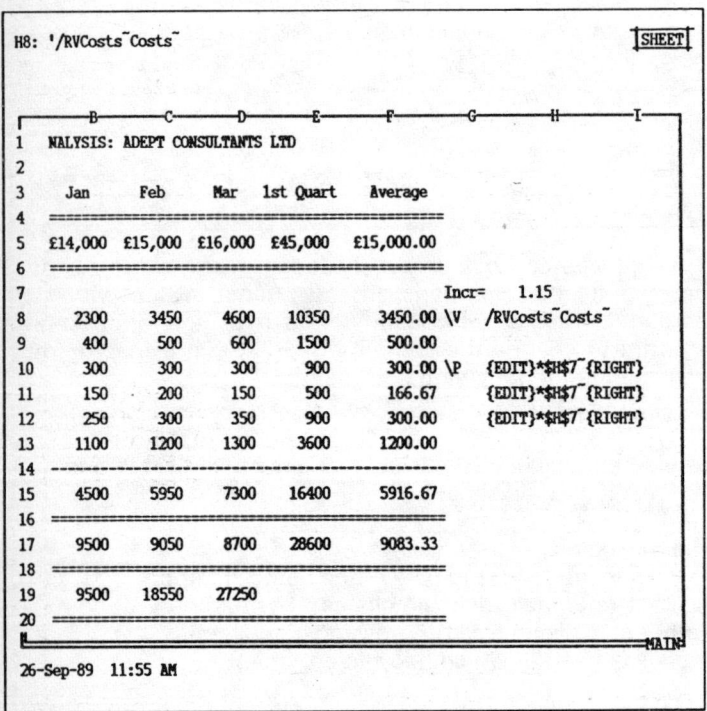

A final addition to the above macros could be made to allow for user entry of the 'increment' value from the keyboard, rather than having to edit cell H7. This can be achieved by the use of the GETNUMBER macro command, which allows the user to enter a number which is then inserted into the specified cell in the worksheet. The general format of this macro command is:

{GETNUMBER prompt-string,location}

Other available macro commands are listed in Appendix C. In our particular case, the GETNUMBER command takes the following form:

{GETNUMBER "Enter increment ",H7}~

which is typed into cell H9. Don't forget to use the {**Menu**} **R**ange **N**ame **C**reate command to redefine macro \V to its new range, which now should be H8..H12. Save the resulting worksheet under the filename MACRO3, before using it. Your screen should now display the following:

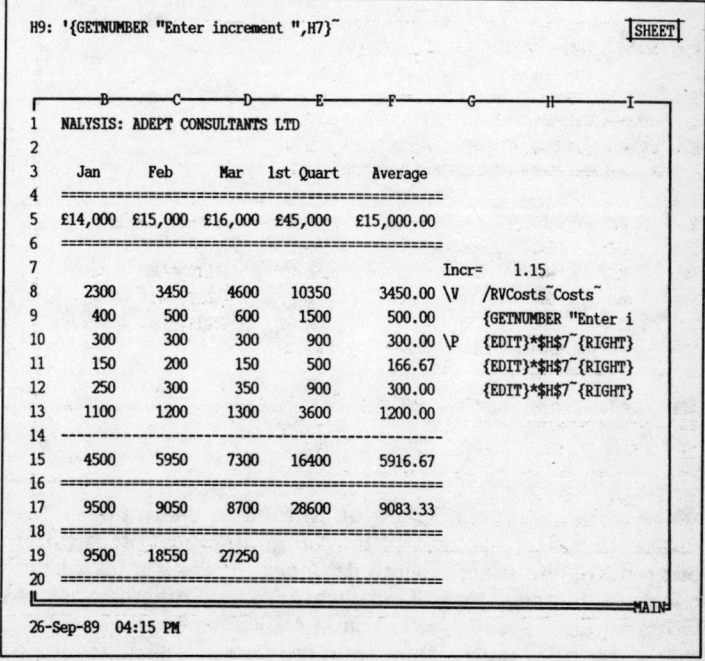

```
H9: '{GETNUMBER "Enter increment ",H7}~                                    |SHEET|


     B        C        D        E          F        G        H          I
 1  NALYSIS: ADEPT CONSULTANTS LTD
 2
 3   Jan      Feb      Mar    1st Quart   Average
 4  ================================================
 5  £14,000  £15,000  £16,000 £45,000    £15,000.00
 6  ================================================
 7                                       Incr=    1.15
 8   2300     3450     4600    10350     3450.00 \V  /RVCosts~Costs~
 9    400      500      600     1500      500.00     {GETNUMBER "Enter i
10    300      300      300      900      300.00 \P  {EDIT}*$H$7~{RIGHT}
11    150      200      150      500      166.67     {EDIT}*$H$7~{RIGHT}
12    250      300      350      900      300.00     {EDIT}*$H$7~{RIGHT}
13   1100     1200     1300     3600     1200.00
14  ------------------------------------------------
15   4500     5950     7300    16400     5916.67
16  ================================================
17   9500     9050     8700    28600     9083.33
18  ================================================
19   9500    18550    27250
20  ================================================
                                                                      |MAIN|

26-Sep-89   04:15 PM
```

81

As a second example, use the {**Menu**} **R**ange **N**ame **C**reate command to name the cell block A1..F20 as 'Analysis', then write a macro that will print to the printer the specified range name. Remember that to print the named range manually you would require to issue the {**Services**} **P**rint **S**ettings **S**ource **R**ange command, then type the range to be printed and press <Enter> to confirm the range selection, followed by **A**lign **G**o **Q**uit.

Finally, as an example of a macro which incorporates range names and an error routine, the file MACRO3 has been added to as shown below.

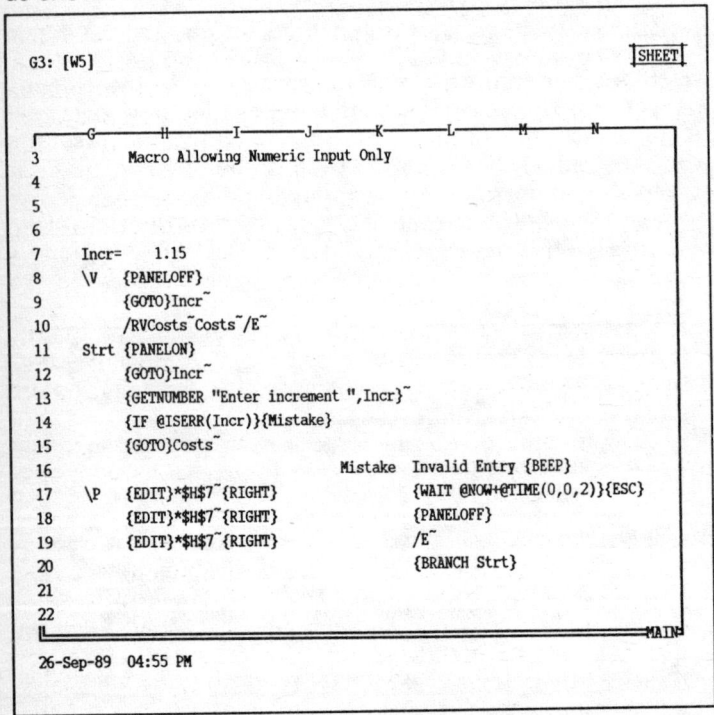

```
G3: [W5]                                              |SHEET|

     G      H       I      J       K       L      M      N
 3           Macro Allowing Numeric Input Only
 4
 5
 6
 7    Incr=    1.15
 8    \V  {PANELOFF}
 9        {GOTO}Incr~
10        /RVCosts~Costs~/E~
11    Strt {PANELON}
12        {GOTO}Incr~
13        {GETNUMBER "Enter increment ",Incr}~
14        {IF @ISERR(Incr)}{Mistake}
15        {GOTO}Costs~
16                            Mistake  Invalid Entry {BEEP}
17    \P  {EDIT}*$H$7~{RIGHT}          {WAIT @NOW+@TIME(0,0,2)}{ESC}
18        {EDIT}*$H$7~{RIGHT}          {PANELOFF}
19        {EDIT}*$H$7~{RIGHT}          /E~
20                                     {BRANCH Strt}
21
22                                                        MAIN
26-Sep-89  04:55 PM
```

When writing macros it is a good idea to use range names throughout. This allows you to change the location of certain portions of the macro without having to keep track of, and change references to, cell addresses. Also, a macro should be written in such a way as to anticipate any mistakes that might be made by the user. This requires error checking to be incorporated into it so that it provides for the possible reentry of

82

data, rather than causing an abrupt exit from the particular application.

With this in mind, the above macro checks to see if an error results from a non-numeric entry, and if so, it causes the internal speaker to bleep, and asks for data reentry. If all is well, the macro causes the cursor to be placed at the beginning of the 'Costs' range so that you can choose which of the various cost categories you would like to update by activating macro \P. Before you run the amended macro, save it under the filename MACRO4.

Learn Mode:

Symphony provides an easy method of entering repetitive keystroke type macros into a worksheet - the Learn Mode. Before this can be used a learn range has to be specified in an unused section of the sheet using the {**Services**} **S**ettings **L**earn **R**ange command sequence, highlight a suitable range, and press **Q**uit twice to return to the 'SHEET' mode.

To activate automatic macro storage, press the {Learn} key (Alt-F5). The 'LEARN' indicator light stays on at the bottom of the screen while macro recording is in progress. With this light on every key you press is recorded in the learn range. Press {Learn} again to toggle off this mode.

If you look at the learn range now you will see all the instructions for a macro already typed out. This must of course be named in the usual manner (as discussed previously), before the macro can be used.

As an exercise use the 'LEARN' mode to create another macro to save your worksheet, and compare the results with your manually generated one.

Macro Keys:

Most keystrokes can be manually entered in a macro by typing the appropriate key. All the special macro keys must be typed as shown in the list below. In addition all special keys (with the exception of the <Enter> key) must be enclosed in braces. You can use upper- or lower-case letters when entering the special key names. Some keys only function in one of the environments, as noted below.

Macro Key	Description
~	Enter key
{~}	Tilde appears as ~
{{} and {}}	Braces appear as { and }
{ABS}	Inserts the absolute character ($) in cell range addresses (Sheet)

83

{AUTO}	Turns auto justification on/off (Doc)
{BEGIN}	Calls up print attribute menu (Doc)
{BIGLEFT}	Move left one screen
{BIGRIGHT}	Move right one screen
{BS}	Backspace key, erases character to left of cursor. If a range is selected, erases current range
{BREAK}	Sends a signal to a remote computer signaling it to stop sending data and to wait for instructions (Comm)
{CALC}	Recalculates all formulae in the worksheet (Sheet)
{CAPTURE}	Switches between capturing and not capturing information in a range and on a printer (Comm)
{CASE}	Changes case of current character (Doc)
{CENTER}	Centres the current line between the left and right margins (Doc)
{COPY}	Copies text (Doc)
{DEL}	Deletes character at the cursor
{DLEFT}	Deletes previous word (Doc)
{DLINE}	Deletes current line (Doc)
{DOWN}	Down arrow key.
{DRAW}	Updates all windows.
{DRIGHT}	Deletes text to end of line (Doc)
{DWORD}	Deletes previous word (Doc)
{EDIT}	Places highlighted entry on the control panel for editing (Sheet)
{END}	End key
{ERASE}	Erases specified block of text (Doc)
{ESC}	Esc key
{FORMAT}	Inserts a format line (Doc)
{GOTO}	Moves pointer to a specified cell or rangename (Sheet)
{HELP}	Provides help during a Symphony session
{HOME}	Home key
{INDENT}	Indents text for current paragraph (Doc)
{INSERT}	Switches between insert and overstrike modes (Doc)
{JUSTIFY}	Justifies the current paragraph (Doc)
{LEFT}	Left arrow key
{MENU}	Displays menu for current window, or {/}
{MERGE}	Inserts merge character (Doc)
{MOVE}	Moves text (Doc)

{NEXTPAGE}	Move cursor to top of next page (Doc)
{PAGE}	Inserts a new page break (Doc)
{PASTE}	Pastes text (Doc)
{PGDN}	PgDn key
{PGUP}	PgUp key
{REPLACE}	Replaces text with specified text (Doc)
{RIGHT}	Right arrow key
{SEARCH}	Searches for specified text (Doc)
{SERVICES}	Displays a menu of general Symphony services
{SPLIT}	Pushes text following the curser down one line
{STOP}	Ends text attribute (Doc)
{SWITCH}	Returns window to previous type
{TAB}	In insert mode inserts spaces up to next tab stop. In overstrike mode moves cursor to next tab (Doc)
{TOPPAGE}	Moves cursor to top of page (Doc)
{TYPE}	Displays a menu of window types
{UP}	Up arrow key
{WHERE}	Displays what the current print page and line number would be (Doc)
{WINDOW}	Switches pointer between active windows
{ZOOM}	Expands a window to full size, or shrinks it to its original size.

To specify two or more consecutive uses of the same key, use a repetition factor within the braces. For example,

> {RIGHT 2}   causes the cell pointer to move right twice.

Debugging a Macro:

Writing macros can lead to mistakes which you must find and correct. To help you with this task, Symphony provides the 'STEP' mode which allows you to check the execution of your macro step by step. Using this technique, you can see exactly what the macro is doing and where it is going wrong.

To invoke the 'STEP' mode press the {Step} key (Alt-F7). The status indicator at the bottom of the worksheet will display the word STEP. If a macro is now invoked, the status indicator changes to 'PAUSE'. The execution of the macro is now paused after processing each of its keystrokes. Pressing any key will execute the next keystroke in the macro. When the end of the macro is reached, the status indicator changes back to 'STEP'.

If you press {Step} again, the status indicator disappears and any macros you may invoke after that will execute normally.

*   *   *

Symphony has many more commands and functions which can be used to build and run your application in special ways. What this book has tried to do is to introduce you to the overall subject and give the beginner a solid foundation on which to build future knowledge.

*   *   *

APPENDIX A—INDICATORS

Indicators are highlighted words that appear either in the top right-hand corner of Symphony's control panel, or at the bottom of the screen, There are three types of indicators: Mode, Status, and Window.

Mode Indicators:
Mode indicators appear during every operation of Symphony at the top right-hand corner of the screen. They inform the user of the current state or condition of Symphony's operation. The table below lists all the mode indicators with their associated description.

Indicator	Description
APP	The current window has been created by an add-in
CRIT	The current criterion record is being edited
EDIT	The current entry is being edited or needs to be edited
ERROR	An error has occurred. To clear it, press \<Esc\> or \<Enter\>
FILES	A menu of files is being displayed
FIND	A Query Find operation is in progress
HELP	The help facility has been invoked
LABEL	A label is being entered
MENU	A command menu is being displayed
NAMES	A menu of existing range names or graph names is being displayed
POINT	The highlighted bar is pointing to a cell or a range of cells
VALUE	A number or formula is being entered
WAIT	A command or process is being executed

Status Indicators:
Status indicators appear at the bottom right-hand corner of the screen and inform the user of the particular condition of the program or a key. For example, CALC indicates that the worksheet's formulae need to be recalculated, while CAPS indicates that the 'Caps Lock' key is on. The table below lists all the status indicators and gives their description.

Indicator	*Description*
Calc	The worksheet's formulae need to be recalculated; press the {CALC} key (F8)
Caps	The <Caps Lock> key is on
Capture	Symphony is logging communications environment activity to the Capture range or the printer
Circ	The worksheet contains a formula that refers to itself (occurs only when the recalculation order is 'Natural')
Draw	One or more windows need to be updated; press the {**Draw**} key (**Alt-F8**)
End	The <End> key is on
Learn	Keystrokes are being stored in the {**Learn**} range (**Alt-F5**) to create a macro
Macro	A macro is being executed
Mem	Less than 4096 bytes of memory is available
New Record	A new record is being entered in a 'FORM' environment
Num	The <Num Lock> key is on
OnLine	Connection has been established with a remote computer
Ovr	In word processing, indicates that the overstrike mode is on; press the <Ins> key to change this
Pause	A macro is executing in single-step mode; press a key to continue
Scroll	The <Scroll Lock> key is on
Step	The {**STEP**} mode (**Alt-F7**) has been activated; a macro is executing one step at a time
User	The {**USER**} key (**F7**) is on; you can enter the name of a macro

Window Indicators:
The Window indicators inform the user of Symphony's current window type. The table below lists all the window indicators with their associated description.

Indicator	Description
COMM	Communications window type
DOC	Word processing window type
FORM	Forms-oriented database window type
GRAPH	Graphics window type
SHEET	Worksheet window type

APPENDIX B—@FUNCTIONS

Lotus Symphony's @functions are built-in formulae that perform specialised calculations. Their general format is:

```
@name(arg1,arg2,...)
```

where 'name' is the function name, and 'arg1', 'arg2', etc, are the arguments required for the evaluation of the function. Arguments must appear in a parenthesized list as shown above and their exact number depends on the function being used. However, there are seven functions that do not require arguments and are used without parentheses. These are: @ERR, @FALSE, @NA, @NOW, @PI, @RAND and @TRUE.

There are three types of arguments used with @functions: numeric values, range values and string values, the type used being dependent on the type of function. Numeric value arguments can be entered either directly as numbers, as a cell address, a cell range name or as a formula. Range value arguments can be entered either as a range address or a range name, while string value arguments can be entered as an actual value (a string in double quotes), as a cell address, as a cell name or a formula.

Types of Functions:
There are several types of functions, such as mathematical, logical, financial, statistical, string, date and time, special, and database statistical. Each type requires their own number and type of arguments. These are listed below under the various function categories.

Mathematical Functions:
Mathematical functions evaluate a result using numeric arguments. The various functions and their meanings are as follows:

Function	Description
@ABS(X)	Returns the absolute value of X
@ACOS(X)	Returns the angle in radians, whose cosine is X (arc cosine of X)
@ASIN(X)	Returns the angle in radians, whose sine is X (arc sine of X)
@ATAN(X)	Returns the angle in radians, between $\pi/2$ and $-\pi/2$, whose tangent is X (arc tangent of X - 2 quadrant)
@ATAN2(X,Y)	Returns the angle in radians, between π and $-\pi$, whose tangent is Y/X (arc tangent of Y/X - 4 quadrant)

@COS(X)	Returns the cosine of angle X, (X must be in radians)
@EXP(X)	Raises e to the power of X
@INT(X)	Returns the integer part of X
@LN(X)	Returns the natural logarithm (base e) of X
@LOG(X)	Returns the logarithm (base 10) of X
@MOD(X,Y)	Returns the remainder of X/Y
@PI	Returns the value of π (3.1415926)
@RAND	Returns a random number between 0 and 1
@ROUND(X,N)	Returns the value of X rounded to N places
@SIN(x)	Returns the sine of angle X (X must be in radians)
@SQRT(X)	Returns the square root of X
@TAN(X)	Returns the tangent of angle X (X must be in radians).

Logical Functions:

Logical functions produce a value based on the result of a conditional statement, using numeric arguments. The various functions and their meanings are as follows:

Function	*Description*
@FALSE	Returns the logical value 0
@IF(Cr,X,Y)	Returns the value X if Cr is TRUE and Y if Cr is FALSE
@ISERR(X)	Returns 1 (TRUE) if X contains ERR, else returns 0 (FALSE)
@ISNA(X)	Returns 1 (TRUE) if X contains NA, else returns 0 (FALSE)
@ISNUMBER(X)	Returns 1 (TRUE) if X contains a numeric value, else returns 0 (FALSE)
@ISSTRING(X)	Returns 1 (TRUE) if X contains a string value, else returns 0 (FALSE)
@TRUE	Returns the logical value 1.

Financial Functions:

Financial functions evaluate loans, annuities, and cash flows over a period of time, using numeric arguments. The various functions and their meanings are as follows:

Function	Description
@CTERM(Rt,Fv,Pv)	Returns the number of compounding periods for an investment of present value Pv, to grow to a future value Fv, at a fixed interest rate Rt
@DDB(Ct,Sg,Lf,Pd)	Returns the double-declining depreciation allowance of an asset, given the original cost Ct, predicted salvage value Sg, the life Lf of the asset, and the period Pd
@FV(Pt,Rt,Tm)	Returns the future value of a series of equal payments, each of equal amount Pt, earning a periodic interest rate Rt, over a number of payment periods in term Tm
@IRR(Gs,Rg)	Returns the internal rate of return of the series of cash flows in a range Rg, based on the approximate percentage guess Gs of the IRR
@NPV(Rt,Rg)	Returns the present value of the series of future cash flows in range Rg, discounted at a periodic interest rate Rt
@PMT(Pl,Rt,Tm)	Returns the amount of the periodic payment needed to pay off the principal Pl, at a periodic interest rate Rt, over the number of payment periods in term Tm
@PV(Pt,Rt,Tm)	Returns the present value of a series of equal payments, each of equal amount Pt, discounted at a periodic interest rate Rt, over a number of payment periods in term Tm
@RATE(Fv,Pv,Tm)	Returns the periodic interest rate necessary for a present value Pv to grow to a future value Fv, over the number of compounding periods in term Tm
@SLN(Ct,Sg,Lf)	Returns the straight-line depreciation allowance of an asset for one period, given the original cost Ct, predicted salvage value Sg, and the life Lf of the asset

| @SYD(Ct,Sg,Lf,Pd) | Returns the sum-of-the-years' digits depreciation allowance of an asset, given the original cost Ct, predicted salvage value Sg, the life Lf of the asset, and the period Pd |
| @TERM(Pt,Rt,Fv) | Returns the number of payment periods of an investment, given the amount of each payment Pt, the periodic interest rate Rt, and the future value of the investment Fv. |

Statistical Functions:

Statistical functions evaluate lists of values using numeric arguments or cell ranges. The various functions and their meaning are as follows:

Function	Description
@AVG(Rg)	Returns the average of values in range Rg
@COUNT(Rg)	Returns the number of non-blank entries in range Rg
@MAX(Rg)	Returns the maximum value in range Rg
@MIN(Rg)	Returns the minimum value in range Rg
@STD(Rg)	Returns the standard deviation of values in range Rg
@SUM(Rg)	Returns the sum of values in range Rg
@VAR(Rg)	Returns the variance of values in range Rg.

String Functions:

String functions operate on strings and produce numeric or string values dependent on the function.

Function	Description
@CHAR(X)	Returns the ASCII character that corresponds to the code number X
@CLEAN(Sg)	Removes control characters from string Sg
@CODE(Sg)	Returns the ASCII code number for the first character in string Sg

@EXACT(Sg1,Sg2)	Returns 1 (TRUE) if strings Sg1 and Sg2 are exactly alike, otherwise 0 (FALSE)
@FIND(Ss,Sg,Sn)	Returns position at which the first occurrence of search string Ss begins in string Sg, starting the search from search number Sn
@LEFT(Sg,N)	Returns the first (leftmost) N characters in string Sg
@LENGTH(Sg)	Returns the number of characters in string Sg
@LOWER(Sg)	Returns all lower case letters in string Sg
@MID(Sg,Sn,N)	Returns N characters from string Sg beginning with the character at Sn
@N(Rg)	Returns the numeric value in the upper left corner cell in range Rg
@PROPER(Sg)	Returns all words in string Sg with first letter in uppercase and the rest in lowercase
@REPEAT(Sg,N)	Returns string Sg N times
@REPLACE(O,S,N,Ns)	Removes N characters from original string O, starting at character S and then inserts new string Ns in the vacated place
@RIGHT(Sg,N)	Returns the last (rightmost) N characters in string Sg
@S(Rg)	Returns the string value in the upper left corner cell in range Rg
@STING(X,N)	Returns the numeric value X as a string, with N decimal places
@TRIM(Sg)	Returns string Sg with no leading, trailing or contiguous spaces
@UPPER(Sg)	Returns all letters in string Sg in uppercase
@VALUE(Sg)	Returns the numeric value of string Sg.

Date and Time Functions:

Date and time functions generate and use serial numbers to represent dates and times. Each date between 1 January 1900 and 31 December 2099 has an integer serial number starting with 1 and ending with 73050. Each moment during a day has a decimal serial number starting with 0.000 at midnight and ending with 0.99999 just before the following midnight. Thus the value 0.5 indicates midday. The various functions and their meaning are as follows:

Function	Description
@DATE(Yr,Mh,Dy)	Returns the date number of Yr,Mh,Dy
@DATEVALUE(Ds)	Returns the date number of date string Ds
@DAY(Dn)	Returns the day number of date number Dn
@HOUR(Tn)	Returns the hour number of time number Tn
@MINUTE(Tn)	Returns the minute number of time number Tn
@MONTH(Dn)	Returns the month number of date number Dn
@NOW	Returns the serial number for the current date and time
@SECOND(Tn)	Returns the second number of time number Tn
@TIME(Hr,Ms,Ss)	Returns the time number of Hr,Ms,Ss
@TIMEVALUE(Ts)	Returns the time number of time string Ts
@YEAR(Dn)	Returns the year number of date number Dn.

Special Functions:
Special functions perform a variety of advanced tasks, such as looking up a value in a table. The various functions and their meaning are as follows:

Function	Description
@@(Ca)	Returns the contents of the cell referenced by cell address Ca
@CELL(At,Rg)	Returns the code representing the attribute At of range Rg
@CELLPOINTER(At)	Returns the code representing the attribute At of the highlighted cell
@CHOOSE(X,V0,..,Vn)	Returns the Xth value in the list V0,..,Vn
@COLS(Rg)	Returns the number of columns in the range Rg

@ERR	Returns the value of ERR
@HLOOKUP(X,Rg,Rn)	Performs a horizontal table look-up by comparing the value X to each cell in the top row, or index row, in range Rg, then moves down the column in which a match is found by the specified row number Rn
@INDEX(Rg,Cn,Rw)	Returns the value of the cell in range at the intersection of column Cn and row Rw
@NA	Returns the numeric value of NA
@ROW(Rg)	Returns the number of row in range Rg
@VLOOKUP(X,Rg,Cn)	Performs a vertical table look-up by comparing the value X to each cell in the first column, or index column, in range Rg, then moves across the row in which a match is found by the specified column number Cn.

Database Statistical Functions:

Database statistical functions perform statistical calculations on a database. The database, which is called the input range, consists of records, which include fields and field names. A criterion range must be setup to select the records from the database that each function uses. The various functions and their meaning are as follows:

Function	*Description*
@DAVG(Ip,Of,Cr)	Returns the average of the values in the offset column Of, of the input range Ip that meet the criteria in the criterion range Cr
@DCOUNT(Ip,Os,Cr)	Returns the number of non-blank cells in the offset column Os, of the input range Ip that meet the criteria in the criterion range Cr
@DMAX(Ip,Os,Cr)	Returns the maximum value in the offset column Os, of the input range Ip that meet the criteria in the criterion range Cr

@DMIN(Ip,Os,Cr)	Returns the minimum value in the offset column Os, of the input range Ip that meet the criteria in the criterion range Cr
@DSTD(Ip,Os,Cr)	Returns the standard deviation of the values in the offset column Os, of the input range Ip that meet the criteria in the criterion range Cr
@DSUM(Ip,Os,Cr)	Returns the sum of the values in the offset column Os, of the input range Ip that meet the criteria in the criterion range Cr
@DVAR(Ip,Os,Cr)	Returns the variance of the values in the offset column Os, of the input range Ip that meet the criteria in the criterion range Cr.

APPENDIX C—MACRO COMMANDS

There are a number of macro commands available in Symphony each one of which has a specified syntax. This takes one of the following two forms:

```
{Keyword}
{Keyword arg1,arg2,...,argn}
```

and must be typed into a macro with the prescribed number of arguments. Uppercase and lowercase letters are equivalent in macro keywords and are, therefore, interchangeable. However, it is a good idea to always use a different case for macro commands from that of range names. In the examples given in this book, all macro commands are entered in uppercase, while range names are entered in lowercase. This makes it easier to distinguish between the two.

Note that incorrect macro commands result in an error when the macro is invoked, and not when the macro command is entered. Also, note that there is an important difference between macros and @functions. If you place your macros in any place other than their own window, any command that disrupts the sheet layout, such as Menu Move, Menu Insert, or Menu Delete, will cause the macro to fail. One way of overcoming this problem, is to always use range names to refer to all individual cells, as well as ranges, in a worksheet.

Some macro commands, such as GETNUMBER, change the contents of cells in the worksheet. However, Symphony may not always update or recalculate the worksheet after each macro command is executed. Normally, the inclusion of a tilde (˜), which executes an <Enter> at the end of a command accomplishes this, while others require the inclusion of the {CALC} command. In the following list a superscripted C (^{C}) against a command indicates that a {CALC} command must be used, while a tilde (˜) indicates that a ˜ command must be used, before the worksheet is updated.

?	{?} stops macro execution temporarily for keyboard input
AUTO	{AUTO} turns auto-justification on/off
BEEP	{BEEP <Num>} causes the speaker to bleep. Num is an optional number from 1 to 4 used for different tones (the default value is 1)
BEGIN	{BEGIN} calls up the Print Attribute menu

BLANK	{BLANK Loc} erases the contents of a specified cell location given by Loc or a range of cells such as A1..A9
BRANCH	{BRANCH Loc} causes macro execution to branch to a different location
BREAKOFF	{BREAKOFF} disables the BREAK key during macro execution
BREAKON	{BREAKON} enables normal BREAK key function
CASE	{CASE} changes case of current character
CLOSE	{CLOSE} closes a file that has been opened with the OPEN command
CONTENTS^c	{CONTENTS Dest,Sour,<Wdth>, <Frmt>} places the contents of Source cell, if a 'string', into Destination cell as a label. If the contents of the Source cell are numeric and the optional arguments of Width and Format are different from those of the Source cell, then Symphony takes the number in Source together with specified Width and Format and stores it as a left-aligned label in Destination cell
COPY	{COPY} copies text
DEFINE^c	{DEFINE Loc1:Type1,Loc2:Type2,..} specifies Location cells and declares Types of arguments to be passed to a subroutine
DISPATCH	{DISPATCH Loc} branches indirectly to the specified destination, given by Loc
DLEFT	{DLEFT} deletes text to beginning of current line
DLINE	{DLINE} deletes current line
DRIGHT	{DRIGHT} deletes text to end of current line
DWORD	{DWORD} deletes previous word

FILESIZE^C	{FILESIZE Loc} determines the number of bytes in a currently opened file and places it in specified Location
FOR	{FOR Count,Start,Stop,Step,Startloc} executes repeatedly the macro subroutine that begins at the Start location. Count is a cell in which Symphony holds the current number of repetition, while Startloc is the first cell, or range name of which subroutine to be executed
FORBREAK	{FORBREAK} cancels execution of current FOR loop
FORMAT	{FORMAT} inserts format line
GET^C	{GET Loc} stops macro execution temporarily and stores a single character you type in a specified cell given by Loc
GETLABEL	{GETLABEL Prompt,Loc} stops macro execution temporarily, prompts you with Prompt string and stores the characters you type as a label in a specified cell given by Loc
GETNUMBER	{GETNUMBER Prompt,Loc} stops macro execution temporarily, prompts you with Prompt string and stores the characters you type as a number in a specified cell given by Loc
GETPOS^C	{GETPOS Loc} determines the current position of the file pointer in an open file and displays it in Loc
HANDSHAKE	{HANDSHAKE Ss,Rs,Tov,Caploc} sends a string (Ss) to a remote computer, waits a specified time (Tov) for the receive-string (Rs), places any response in a capture-location (Caploc), and branches depending on the success of the exchange
IF	{IF Condition_command} conditionally executes the command that follows the IF command

INDICATE	{INDICATE <String>} changes the mode indicator. The String argument is optional
LET⁻	{LET Loc,String} stores an entered label or {LET Loc,Num} stores an entered number, in a specified cell given by Loc
LOOK^C	{LOOK Loc} scans the keyboard for input during macro execution and stores that character in Loc
MENUBRANCH	{MENUBRANCH Loc} stops macro execution to allow selection from a customized menu with user-defined choices. The upper left-corner of the menu is given by Loc
MENUCALL	{MENUCALL Loc} stops macro execution to allow menu selection and executes the corresponding macro as a subroutine. The upper left-corner of the menu is given by Loc
MERGE	{MERGE} inserts merge character
MOVE	{MOVE} moves text
NEXTPAGE	{NEXTPAGE} moves cursor to top of next page
ONERROR^C	{ONERROR Loc,<Msg>} branches to Loc if an error occurs during macro execution. The usual error message can be optionally recorded in Msg
OPEN	{OPEN Filename,Mode} opens the specified file in the current directory for reading or writing. Mode is a single character (R for Reading, W for Write or M for Modify) which describes the type of file access
PAGE	{PAGE} inserts a new page break
PANELOFF	{PANELOFF} disables redrawing of control panel during macro execution
PANELON	{PANELON} enables control panel redrawing
PASTE	{PASTE} pastes text
PHONE	{PHONE Phonenumber} places a call to a specific number. You can specify a string-value expression as the argument

102

PUT^C	{PUT Loc,Col,Row,String} puts a string or {PUT Loc,Col,Row,Num} puts a number, in the specified Location within a specified range
QUIT	{QUIT} terminates macro execution and returns control to the keyboard
READ^C	{READ Bytes,Loc} reads a number of bytes (characters) from a file into a cell specified by Loc
READLN^C	{READLN Loc} copies a line of characters from the currently open file into the specified location
RECALC	{RECALC Loc,<Condit>,<Iternum>} recalculates the formulae in a specified range, row by row. Condit and Iternum are optional arguments; Condit is evaluated after the range Location is calculated and if Condit is FALSE, it calculates the range again; Iternum specifies the number of times the range is calculated
RECALCCOL	{RECALCCOL Loc,<Condit>,<Iternum>} Recalculates the formulae in a specified range, column by column under the same conditions as RECALC
REPLACE	{REPLACE} replaces text with specified text
RESTART	{RESTART} cancels the subroutine and clears the subroutine stack
RETURN	{RETURN} returns from a subroutine
SEARCH	{SEARCH} searches for specific text
SETPOS	{SETPOS Pointer} sets the file Pointer in the currently opened file into a new position
STOP	{STOP} ends text attributes
subrout_name	{subrout_name} calls a subroutine
TOPPAGE	{TOPPAGE} moves cursor to top of current page
WAIT	{WAIT Timenum} suspends macro execution for a specified time

WINDOWSOFF	{WINDOWSOFF} disables redrawing the display screen during macro execution
WINDOWSON	{WINDOWSON} enables normal screen redrawing
WRITE	{WRITE String} copies characters into an open file
WRITELN	{WRITELN String} Adds a carriage-return line-feed sequence to a string of characters and writes the string to a file.

INDEX

NOTES

NOTES

NOTES

NOTES

NOTES